SPANIS
POCKET

A Headway phrasebook

Rosa María Martín

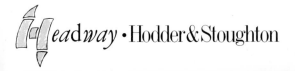

Headway · Hodder & Stoughton

British Library Cataloguing in Publication Data
Martin, Rosa Maria
  Spanish in your pocket.
  1. Spanish language. Usage
  I. Title
  468

ISBN 0 340 50912 0

First published 1990

Second impression 1990

Typeset by Wearside Tradespools, Fulwell, Sunderland
Printed and bound in Hong Kong for Hodder and Stoughton
Limited, Mill Road, Dunton Green, Sevenoaks, Kent by
Colorcraft Ltd.

Contents

Introduction

This book is an essential accessory for visitors to Spain and other Spanish-speaking countries, of whatever age and for whatever purpose. It provides a thorough survival guide with useful phrases in authentic but simple modern Spanish, in clearly defined logical sections for quick and easy reference. Features include:

- Up-to-date information sections about modern Spanish life.
- A full alphabetical wordlist for quick reference.
- A simple, consistent and effective pronunciation guide.
- Key root sentences and phrases suitable for a variety of situations through substitution of appropriate vocabulary.
- Simple and effective questions to obtain short answers, avoiding confusion.
- Suggestions for some of the answers you might hear in response to your questions.
- A special general information reference section making this much more than just a phrase book.
- A section of basic expressions suitable for many situations.

In Spanish there is a difference between 'you' used formally (*Usted*) and informally (*tú*). Phrases and expressions employing one or the other are clearly indicated, and where both are suitable, both options are given.

Generally, Spanish nouns end in **o** for masculine nouns (*el*) and in **a** for feminine nouns (*la*). Where this is not the case, the wordlist section indicates clearly by the symbol **m** or **f** after the word in question.

You can prepare yourself before your visit by practising a number of the more common basic expressions and becoming familiar with Spanish pronunciation patterns outlined in the book, although it can be equally effective when used 'on site'.

¡Buen Viaje!

Pronunciation

Spanish pronunciation is very straightforward: everything is pronounced, and letters keep the same values. The following guide is used to indicate pronunciation that differs from English.

Symbol		Spanish Word		English Word
I	as in	hay	compare with	I
a		padre		pat
air		reserva		fair
e		tengo		tent
ee		vida		me
eh		doble		bled
o		quiero		low
oo		uva		soon
y		habitación		yes
b		baño		*see below*
v		lavabo		
ch		plancha		church
g		gato		get
h		jabón		*see below*
k		cama		cat
r		querer		*see below*
s		estrella		glass
th		cerca		thick

- **b** and **v** sound the same in Spanish. At the beginning of a word or syllable, both are pronounced like English **b** as in 'big'. In the middle of a word, it is a softer sound. In the following phrases the symbol **b** will be used for both sounds.
- **g** is sometimes and **j** is always pronounced at the back of the throat, like the **ch** in Scottish loch. The symbol **h** is used when this occurs. (Do not confuse this with **eh**. Where the **h** symbol coincides with the **e** symbol, they are separated with a hyphen.)
- **r** is always strongly pronounced: it is rolled like a Scottish **r**.
- Stressed syllables are shown in bold.

Basic expressions

yes	sí *see*
no	no *no*
please	por favor *por fabbor*
thank you	gracias *grath-yas*
that's enough	basta *basta*
I don't know	no sé *no seh*
I'm sorry/excuse me	perdón *pairdon*
I'm (very) sorry	lo siento (mucho) *lo see-yento (moocho)*
excuse me (to get attention)	oiga, por favor *oyga, por fabbor*
Mr/Sir	Señor *senyor*
Mrs/Madam	Señora *senyora*
Miss	Señorita *senyoreeta*
just a moment	un momento *oon momento*
I (don't) like it	(no) me gusta *(no) meh goosta*
I (don't) want it	(no) lo quiero *(no) lo kee-yerro*
How much is it?	¿Cuánto es? *kwanto es?*

- For basic greetings etc, see page 59.

ARRIVAL AND DEPARTURE

At the border

- Spain has the same customs regulations as other EEC member countries. For details of allowances, pick up a leaflet at the border.
- Important signs at airports and borders with road access (*frontera*) are also shown in English. Just follow the signs.
- Visitors under the age of 18 must have written consent from their parents or guardian before they will be allowed into the country.

Where is the customs office?

¿Dónde está la aduana?
dondeh esta la adwana?

I don't understand

No comprendo
no komprendo

Do you speak English

¿Habla inglés?
abla ingles?

I'm here . . .	Vengo . . . *bengo . . .*
. . . on holiday	. . . de vacaciones *deh bakathyon-es*
. . . on business	. . . de negocios *deh negoth-yos*
. . . to visit some friends	. . . a visitar a unos amigos *a beeseetar a oonos ameegos*
. . . for two weeks	. . . para dos semanas *para dos semanas*
. . . for a month	. . . para un mes *para oon mes*
I'll be at this address	Estaré en esta dirección *estareh en esta dirrekth-yon*
We're passing through	Vamos de paso *bamos deh paso*
I've lost my passport	He perdido mi pasaporte *eh pairdeedo mee pasaporteh*
I have nothing to declare	No llevo nada *no yebbo nada*
I've got . . .	Llevo . . . *yebbo . . .*
. . . cigarettes	. . . cigarrillos *theegaree-yos*
. . . drinks	. . . bebidas *bebeedas*
. . . perfume	. . . perfume *pairfoomeh*
. . . this	. . . esto *esto*

Luggage

Where are the trolleys?	¿Dónde están los carros? *dondeh estan los karros?*
I can't find . . .	No encuentro . . . *no enkwentro . . .*
. . . my bag	. . . mi bolsa *mee bolsa*
. . . my luggage	. . . mi equipaje *mee ekeepaheh*
. . . my suitcase	. . . mi maleta *mee maletta*
Could you carry my luggage?	¿Puede llevarme el equipaje? *pwedeh yebbarmeh el ekeepaheh?*
It's this one	Es esto *es esto*
How much do I owe you?	¿Cuánto le debo? *kwanto leh debbo?*

At the information desk

Where is . . . ?	¿Dónde está . . . ? *dondeh esta . . . ?*
. . . the taxi rank	. . . la parada de taxis *la parada deh taxees*
. . . the bus to the city	. . . el autobús a la ciudad *el owtoboos a la theeoodad*
. . . the left luggage office	. . . la consigna *la konseegna*

9

Arrival and Departure

Where can I . . . ?	¿Dónde puedo . . . ? *dondeh pwedo . . . ?*
. . . buy a ticket	. . . comprar un billete *komprar oon beeyeteh*
. . . change money	. . . cambiar dinero *kamb-yar deenero*
. . . hire a car	. . . alquilar un coche *alkeelar oon kocheh*
. . . make a phone call	. . . llamar por teléfono *yamar por telefono*
Could you give me . . . ?	¿Puede darme . . . ? *pwedeh darmeh . . . ?*
. . . a bus timetable	. . . un horario de autobuses *oon orareeo deh owtobooses*
. . . a brochure of (the town)	. . . un folleto de (la ciudad) *oon foyetto deh (la thee-oodad)*
. . . a list of hotels	. . . una lista de hoteles *oona leesta de otel-es*
. . . a train timetable	. . . un horario de trenes *oon orareeo deh tren-es*
Could you find me a . . . hotel?	¿Puede buscarme un hotel . . . ? *pwedeh booskarmeh oon otel . . . ?*
. . . luxury	. . . de lujo *deh loo-ho*
. . . three star	. . . de tres estrellas *deh tres estreyas*
. . . economic/cheap	. . . barato *barato*

Asking the way

Excuse me	` Oiga, por favor *oyga, por fabbor*
How do I get . . . ?	¿Para ir . . . ? *para eer . . . ?*
. . . to Benidorm	. . . a Benidorm *a beneedorm*
. . . to the Hotel (Sol)	. . . al hotel (Sol) *al otel (sol)*
. . . to the beach	. . . a la playa *a la ply-a*
. . . to the airport	. . . al aeropuerto *al aeropwairto*
How many kilometres to (Madrid)?	¿A cuántos kilómetros está (Madrid)? *a kwantos keelometros esta (madreed)?*
Do you have a map/a plan?	¿Tiene un mapa/un plano? *tee-yenneh oon mapa/oon plano?*
Where are the toilets/the shops?	¿Dónde están los servicios/las tiendas? *dondeh estan los sairbeeth-yos/las tee-yendas?*
Is it a long way away/nearby?	¿Está lejos/cerca? *esta leh-hos/thairka?*
Do I have to take the bus/the underground?	¿Tengo que tomar el autobús/el metro? *tengo keh tomar el owtoboos/el metro?*
Can you walk there?	¿Se puede ir a pie? *seh pwedeh eer a pee-yeh?*
Can you go with me?	¿Puede acompañarme? *pwedeh akompanyarmeh?*

11

Arrival and Departure

Where is . . . ?	¿Dónde está . . . ? *dondeh esta . . . ?*
. . . the station	. . . la estación *la estathyon*
. . . the underground station	. . . el metro *el metro*
. . . the train for the airport	. . . el tren para el aeropuerto *el tren para el aeropwairto*
. . . the taxi rank	. . . la parada de taxis *la parada deh taxees*
. . . the motorway to (Bilbao)	. . . la autopista a (Bilbao) *la owtopeesta a (beelbao)*
. . . the (Madrid) road	. . . la carretera de (Madrid) *la karaterra deh (madreed)*
. . . the police station	. . . la Comisaría *la komeesareea*
. . . the tourist office	. . . la oficina de turismo *la ofeetheena deh tooreesmo*
. . . the town centre	. . . el centro *el thentro*
Where is there . . . ?	¿Dónde hay . . . ? *dondeh I . . . ?*
. . . a bank	. . . un banco *oon banko*
. . . a car park	. . . un parking *oon parkin*
. . . a supermarket	. . . un supermercado *oon sooper-mairkado*
. . . a telephone	. . . un teléfono *oon telefono*

You may hear:

la primera (calle) *la preemera (ka-yeh)*	the first (street)
la segunda *la segoonda*	the second
la tercera *la tairthera*	the third
a la derecha *a la derecha*	on the right
a la izquierda *a la eethkee-yairda*	on the left
todo recto *todo rekto*	straight on
allí *ayee*	there
aquí (mismo) *akee (meesmo)*	(just) here
en el semáforo *en el semaforo*	at the traffic lights
al final de la calle *al feenal deh la ka-yeh*	at the end of the street
en la esquina *en la eskeena*	on/at the corner
a (quince) kilómetros *a (keentheh) keelometros*	(15) kms away
a (cinco) minutos *a (theenko) meenootos*	(5) minutes away
tome el desvío *tomeh el desbeeo*	take the diversion
no está lejos *no esta le-hos*	it's not far
está cerca de . . . *esta thairka deh*	it's near . . .

Taxi

- Taxi fares vary from town to town. Taxis for hire show a *libre* sign and at night a green light. When not available they display the sign *completo* and a red light at night.
- There is a basic charge plus a meter which should be visible to the passengers. Extra charges may be made at night or for carrying extra luggage. You are advised to ask for a price if making a long journey.
- Tipping of between 5 and 10% is normal.

Taxi!	¡Taxi! *taxee!*
Could you take me . . . ?	Por favor, lléveme . . . *por fabbor, yebbemeh . . .*
. . . to this address	. . . a esta dirección *a esta dirrekth-yon*
. . . to the airport	. . . al aeropuerto *al aeropwairto*
. . . to the hotel (Sol)	. . . al hotel (Sol) *al otel (sol)*
How much is it to the city/the airport?	¿Cuánto cuesta hasta la ciudad/el aeropuerto? *kwanto kwesta asta la theeoodad/el aeropwairto?*
Could you stop here, please?	Pare aquí, por favor *pareh akee, por fabbor*
Could you . . . ?	¿Puede . . . ? *pwedeh . . . ?*
. . . wait for me	. . . esperarme *esperarmeh*
. . . help me with my cases	. . . ayudarme con las maletas *ayoodarmeh kon las malettas*

- For directions see page 13.

Car hire

- Most of the major car-hire companies are to be found at airports and in the main towns and cities, and brochures are available in English stating conditions and prices. You must be at least twenty-one to hire a car in Spain.

I'd like to hire a small/big car	Quiero alquilar un coche pequeño/grande *kee-yerro alkeelar oon kocheh pekenyo/grandeh*
For today/one week	Para hoy/una semana *para oy/oona semana*
How much is it daily/per kilometre	¿Cuánto es por día/por kilómetro? *kwanto es por deea/por keelometro?*
Do you accept credit cards?	¿Aceptan tarjetas de crédito? *atheptan tarhetas deh kreditto?*
Is insurance/mileage included?	¿Está incluído el seguro/el kilometraje? *esta eenklooeedo el segooro/el keelometraheh?*
I'd like comprehensive insurance	Quiero seguro a todo riesgo *kee-yerro segooro a todo ree-esgo*
Can I leave it in (Madrid)?	¿Puedo dejarlo en (Madrid)? *pwedo deh-harlo en (madreed)?*
Do you want my driving licence?	¿Quiere mi permiso de conducir? *kee-yerreh mee pairmeeso deh kondootheer?*

At the airport

Is there a flight to (Alicante)?	¿Hay un vuelo para (Alicante)? *I oon bwelo para (aleekanteh)?*
A ticket for (London), please	Un billete para (Londres), por favor *oon beeyeteh para (londres), por fabbor*
Do I have to make a connection?	¿Hay que hacer conexión? *I keh athair konex-yon?*
When do I have to check in?	¿Cuándo debo presentarme? *kwando debbo presentarmeh?*
I want to . . . my flight	Quiero . . . mi vuelo *kee-yerro . . . mee bwelo*
. . . confirm	. . . confirmar *konfeermar*
. . . cancel	. . . cancelar *kanthelar*
. . . change	. . . cambiar *kamb-yar*
Where is . . . ?	¿Dónde está . . . ? *dondeh esta . . . ?*
. . . the (Iberia) counter	. . . el mostrador (de Iberia) *el mostrador (deh eebereea)*
. . . the duty free shop	. . . la tienda libre de impuestos *la tee-yenda leebreh deh eempwestos*
Is it delayed?	¿Lleva retraso? *yebba retrasso?*
How much is it delayed?	¿Cuánto retraso hay? *kwanto retrasso I?*
I've missed my plane	He perdido mi avión *eh pairdeedo mee ab-yon*

ACCOMMODATION

Hotel

- Look for these signs:
  - **H** (*Hotel*) followed by 1 to 5 stars
  - **H** (*Hostal*) and **P** (*Pensión*) from 1 to 3 stars
  [*Hostal Residencia* or *Pensión Residencia* indicates that no meals are served.]
  These two usually offer good, cheap accommodation although rooms are not usually equipped with a bathroom.
  - a *Parador* is a state-owned luxury hotel, usually housed in a restored historic building and found in an area of outstanding natural beauty. Suitable as an overnight break for road travellers. Also well-known as excellent restaurants.
- Other types of accommodation:
  - **F** (*Fonda*): cheap and basic
  - *Casa* + name of the owner or *Casa de Huespedes*: guest house

17

- *Camas* (beds) or *Habitaciones* (rooms) usually found in private houses
- *Albergue Juvenil*: youth hostel.
- A list of accommodation facilities can normally be found in the local tourist office. Employees may even help to reserve a place for you. In the high season it is advisable to book in advance.
- Nightly prices (per room and not per person) should be clearly displayed on the back of the door of your room. These are inclusive of tax (*IVA Incluido*). Breakfast is not always included in the price. **NOTE:** breakfast is 'Continental' but 'English Breakfast' may be available in some holiday resorts.
- When registering you will be asked to leave your passport at the desk and to complete a form. Your passport will be returned to you shortly afterwards.
- All hotels and campsites are required by law to keep and produce complaints forms (*Hojas de Reclamaciones*) on request.
- You can ask for an extra bed in a double room. This will cost you a percentage of the price of the room (around 35%).
- Full board (*Pensión Completa*) is usually more economical than taking your meals separately.
- Most hotels accept the main credit cards, but check first.
- Most electrical appliances function with two-pin plugs. These require a special adaptor which you can purchase in Britain. Voltages are 220V in most parts of Spain.

Have you any rooms free?	¿Hay habitaciones libres? *I abeetath-yones leebres?*
I have a reservation	Tengo una reserva *tengo oona resairba*
I would like to make a reservation	Quiero hacer una reserva *kee-yerro athair oona resairba*
My name is . . .	Me llamo. . . *meh yamo. . .*

Accommodation

Is there another hotel nearby?	¿Hay otro hotel cerca? *I otro otel thairka?*
I would like two rooms	Quiero dos habitaciones *kee-yerro dos abeetath-yones*
I would like a single/double room	Quiero una habitación individual/doble *kee-yerro oona abeetath-yon indibeedwal/dobbleh*
I would like a room . . .	Quiero una habitación . . . *kee-yerro oona abeetath-yon . . .*
. . . with a double bed	. . . con una cama doble *kon oona kama dobbleh*
. . . with two beds	. . . con dos camas *kon dos kamas*
. . . for three people	. . . triple *treepleh*
. . . with a cot	. . . con una cuna *kon oona koona*
. . . with a bath	. . . con baño *kon banyo*
. . . with a shower	. . . con ducha *kon doocha*
It's for . . .	Es para . . . *es para . . .*
. . . one night	. . . una noche *oona nocheh*
. . . two nights	. . . dos noches *dos noch-es*
. . . two weeks	. . . dos semanas *dos semanas*

How much is it?	¿Cuánto es? *kwanto es?*
Can you write it down?	¿Puede escribirlo? *pwedeh eskreebeerlo?*
Is there a supplementary charge for another bed?	¿Hay suplemento por otra cama? *I sooplemento por otra kama?*
Does the child pay?	¿El niño paga? *el neenyo paga?*
He/she is . . .	Tiene . . . *tee-yeneh . . .*
. . . six months old	. . . seis meses *seys mes-es*
. . . one year old	. . . un año *oon anyo*
. . . five years old	. . . cinco años *theenko anyos*
Do you accept credit cards?	¿Aceptan tarjetas de crédito? *atheptan tarhetas deh kreditto?*
Can I see the room?	¿Puedo ver la habitación? *pwedo bair la abeetath-yon?*
I will (won't) take it	(No) la tomo *(no) la tomo*
It's . . .	Es . . . *es . . .*
. . . very expensive	. . . muy cara *mwee kara*
. . . too small	. . . demasiado pequeña *demas-yado pekenya*
. . . dark	. . . oscura *oskoora*

Accommodation

I would like another room	Quiero otra habitación *kee-yerro otra abeetath-yon*
Could you take my luggage up?	¿Puede subir el equipaje? *pwedeh soobeer el ekeepaheh?*
Is breakfast included?	¿Está incluido el desayuno? *esta eenklooeedo el desayoono?*

What time is ... ?	¿A qué hora es ... ? *a keh ora es ... ?*
... breakfast	... el desayuno *el desayoono*
... lunch	... la comida *la komeeda*
... dinner	... la cena *la thenna*

---

half board	media pensión *med-ya pens-yon*
full board	pensión completa *pens-yon kompletta*
Could you bring breakfast to my room?	¿Puede traer el desayuno a mi habitación? *pwedeh tryair el desayoono a mee abeetathyon?*
Could you call me ... ?	¿Puede llamarme ... ? *pwedeh yamarmeh ... ?*
... for breakfast	... para el desayuno *para el desayoono*
... at seven o'clock	... a las siete *a las see-yetteh*
Can I have the key (for number 10), please?	Por favor, ¿la llave (de la número 10)? *por fabbor, la yabbeh (deh la noomero dee-eth)?*

Accommodation

Is there . . . ?	¿Hay . . . ? *I . . . ?*
. . . air conditioning	. . . aire acondicionado *I-reh akondeeth-yonado*
. . . a lift	. . . ascensor *asthensor*
. . . a safe	. . . caja fuerte *kaha fwairteh*

Could you give me . . . ?	¿Puede darme . . . ? *pwedeh darmeh . . . ?*
. . . an ashtray	. . . un cenicero *oon theneethero*
. . . another blanket	. . . otra manta *otra manta*
. . . a clothes hanger	. . . una percha *oona paircha*
. . . another pillow	. . . otra almohada *otra almo-ada*
. . . some soap	. . . jabón *habbon*
. . . another towel	. . . otra toalla *otra to-alya*

Could you . . . ?	¿Puede . . . ? *pwedeh . . . ?*
. . . put this in the safe	. . . poner esto en la caja *ponair esto en la kaha*
. . . call a taxi	. . . llamar un taxi *yammar oon taxee*
. . . bring down my luggage	. . . bajar el equipaje *bahar el ekeepaheh*
. . . get the bill ready	. . . preparar la cuenta *preparar la kwenta*

Are there any messages for me?	¿Hay recados para mí? *I rekados para mee?*
Excuse me but there's a mistake	Perdone hay un error *pairdoneh I oon error*
It's wrong	Está mal *esta mal*

Camping

You may see:

Camping	*camp site*
Bungalows	*holiday cabins*
Cabinas	*large caravans*
1, 2, 3 categoria	*1st, 2nd and 3rd class*
De lujo	*luxury*

- It is advisable to book in advance at some of the more popular campsites in high season to avoid disappointment. Write direct to the site or the central campsite reservations office (Federación Española de Campings, Gran Vía 88, Grupo 3, 10°–8 Madrid).
- You can buy a useful camping guide (*Guía de Camping*) in bookshops, kiosks and tourist offices. This guide also gives you a phone number you can ring to reserve places at campsites.
- If you intend to camp out of season, check which campsites are open and when. For many the season runs from May to September. The ones that do open out of season sometimes offer a reduction in price.
- Some campsites hire out tents for use on the same site. If you phone before your arrival they might even put up the tent for you.
- Some campsites will make a charge for electricity and/or hot water. You may have to provide your own cable and plug in some of the less fashionable campsites.

23

- When you arrive, reception will ask you for your passport. This will be returned to you when they have taken information for their records.
- If you are under sixteen you must be accompanied by adults.
- Children under eleven years of age usually pay less.
- If you wish to camp outside an official campsite, make sure you get permission from the landowner.
- No more than three tents may be erected together if you are camping on open ground, and you may stay in one place no more than three days. No more than ten people may camp together during this time. If you wish to extend any of these limits you should contact the *Delegado Provincial*.
- You are not permitted to camp:
    - in dangerous or potentially dangerous places such as river banks or areas prone to flooding
    - on land owned or used by the military or by industry
    - within 150 metres of the main water supply for a town or village
    - within city limits
    - on the side of the road
    - within a kilometre of an existing campsite.

Can one camp here?	¿Se puede acampar aquí? *seh pwedeh akampar akee?*
I have a reservation	Tengo una reserva *tengo oona resairba*
Could I see the camp site?	¿Puedo ver el camping? *pwedo bair el kamping?*
Have you spaces free?	¿Tiene plazas libres? *tee-yenneh plathas leebres?*
Could you write it down/give me a leaflet with the prices?	¿Puede escribirlo/darme un folleto con los precios? *pwedeh eskreebeerlo/darmeh oon foyetto kon los preth-yos?*

Accommodation

I have ...	Tengo ... *tengo ...*
... a small/big tent	... una tienda pequeña/ grande *oona tee-yenda pekenya/ grandeh*
... a caravan	... una caravana *oona karabana*
... a car	... un coche *oon kocheh*
... a motorbike	... una moto *oona moto*
How much is it ... ?	¿Cuánto es ... ? *kwanto es ... ?*
... per person	... por persona *por pairsona*
... for a child	... por un niño *por oon neenyo*
... per day	... por día *por deea*
... for the tent	... por la tienda *por la tee-yenda*
... for the car	... por el coche *por el kocheh*
It's for ...	Es para ... *es para ...*
... two adults	... dos adultos *dos adooltos*
... and a child	... y un niño *ee oon neenyo*
... two nights	... dos noches *dos noch-es*

Accommodation

I prefer to be . . .	Prefiero estar . . . *pref-yerro estar . . .*
. . . in the shade	. . . en la sombra *en la sombra*
. . . near the beach	. . . cerca de la playa *thairka deh la ply-a*
. . . a long way from the road	. . . lejos de la carretera *leh-hos deh la kareterra*
Do you rent/have . . . ?	¿Alquilan/tiene . . . ? *alkeelan/tee-yeneh . . . ?*
. . . tents	. . . tiendas *tee-yendas*
. . . caravans	. . . caravanas *karabanas*
. . . cabins	. . . cabinas *kabeenas*
. . . camping equipment	. . . material de camping *matereeal deh kampeeng*
. . . a refrigerator	. . . una nevera *oona neberra*
. . . a light	. . . un farol *oon farol*
. . . mattresses	. . . colchonetas *kolchonettas*
. . . a broom	. . . una escoba *oona eskoba*
. . . butane gas	. . . gas butano *gas bootano*
. . . a frying pan	. . . una sartén *oona sarten*

For other items, see the Wordlist.

Does the campsite close at night?	¿Cierran el camping por la noche? *thee-yerran el kampeeng por la nocheh?*
At what time?	¿A qué hora? *a keh ora?*

Is/are there . . . ?	¿Hay . . . ? *I . . . ?*
. . . a doctor	. . . médico *medikko*
. . . electricity	. . . conexión eléctrica *konex-yon elektreeka*
. . . a first aid box	. . . botiquín *boteekeen*
. . . ice for sale	. . . venta de hielo *benta deh yelo*
. . . sockets in the washblocks	. . . enchufes en los lavabos *enchoof-es en los lababos*

Where is/are . . . ?	¿Dónde está/están . . . ? *dondeh esta/estan . . . ?*
. . . the ironing room	. . . la sala de plancha *la salla deh plancha*
. . . the rubbish bins	. . . los cubos de basura *los koobos deh basoora*
. . . the (hot water) showers	. . . las duchas (de agua caliente) *las doochas (deh agwa kal-yenteh)*
. . . the toilets	. . . los servicios *los sairbeeth-yos*
At what time is the rubbish collected?	¿A qué hora recogen la basura? *a keh ora rekohen la basoora?*

Apartments

You may see:

Se alquila	*For rent*
Piso	*flat*
Apartamento	*apartment*
Chalet	*chalet*
Casa de campo	*country house*
Urbanización	*residential area*

- Degrees of luxury are indicated by a system of 'key' symbols from 1 to 4, with 4 indicating the better equipped apartments.
- Apartments are usually rented out for a fortnight (*quincena*) or a month.
- Blocks of apartments usually have communal areas (gardens, swimming pools) which are subject to regulations for their use. Make sure you know them.
- The traditional siesta period during the early afternoon is generally observed amongst Spanish holidaymakers. Try to keep the noise down about this time if you are not sleeping.
- Many cookers are equipped with a combination of gas rings and electric rings. Many do not have a grill as we know it.

I would like an apartment . . .	Quiero un apartamento . . . *kee-yerro oon apartamento . . .*
. . . with one bedroom	. . . de un dormitorio *deh oon dormeetor-yo*
. . . for two people	. . . para dos personas *para dos pairsonas*
. . . for a month	. . . para un mes *para oon mes*

Accommodation

What floor is it on?	¿En qué piso está? *en keh peeso esta?*
I prefer the first floor/the top floor	Prefiero el primer piso/último piso *pref-yerro el preemair peeso/ oolteemo peeso*
How many beds are there?	¿Cuántas camas hay? *kwantas kamas I?*
How many bedrooms are there?	¿Cuántos dormitorios hay? *kwantos dormitor-yos I?*

Is ... included?	¿Está incluído/a . . . ? *esta eenklooeedo/a . . . ?*
... everything	... todo *todo*
... the gas	... el gas *el gas*
... the water	... el agua *el agwa*
... electricity	... la electricidad *la elektreetheedad*
... the rubbish collection	... la recogida de basura *la rekoheeda deh basoora*
... the cleaning	... la limpieza *la limp-yetha*

Does it have ... ?	¿Tiene . . . ? *tee-yenneh . . . ?*
... a grill	... parrilla *paree-ya*
... a water heater	... calentador *kalentador*
... central heating	... calefacción *kalefakth-yon*

Accommodation

Is it fully equipped?	¿Está equipado completo? *esta ekeepado kompletto?*
Is it electric/gas?	¿Es eléctrico/de gas? *es elektreeko/deh gas?*

Is/are there . . . ?	¿Hay . . . ? *I . . . ?*
. . . bedclothes	. . . ropa de cama *ropa deh kama*
. . . crockery	. . . vajilla *bahee-ya*
. . . cutlery	. . . cubiertos *koob-yairtos*
. . . any furniture	. . . muebles *mweb-les*
. . . towels	. . . toallas *to-al-yas*
. . . a washing machine	. . . lavadora *labadora*
. . . a (children's) swimming pool	. . . piscina (infantil) *pistheena (infanteel)*

I'm going . . .	Me voy . . . *meh boy . . .*
. . . now	. . . ahora *a-ora*
. . . this afternoon/this evening	. . . esta tarde *esta tardeh*
. . . tomorrow	. . . mañana *man-yana*

The bill, please	La cuenta, por favor *la kwenta por fabbor*

Problems

There isn't any gas/(hot) water	No hay gas/agua (caliente) *no I gas/agwa (kal-yenteh)*
The . . . is not working	. . . no funciona *no foonkth-yona*
The . . . is broken	. . . está roto/a *esta roto/a*
. . . air conditioning	El aire acondicionado . . . *el I-reh akondeeth-yonado . . .*
. . . cooker	La cocina . . . *la kotheena . . .*
. . . light	La luz . . . *la looth . . .*
. . . telephone	El teléfono . . . *el telefono . . .*
. . . basin	El lavabo . . . *el lababo . . .*
. . . sink	El fregadero . . . *el fregadero . . .*
. . . bath	El baño . . . *el banyo . . .*
. . . toilet	El wáter . . . *el batair . . .*
. . . shower	La ducha . . . *la doocha . . .*
Can you repair it?	¿Puede reparalo/la? *pwedeh repararlo/la?*
How much do I owe you?	¿Cuánto le debo? *kwanto leh debbo?*

Accommodation

You may hear:

No hay habitaciones *no I abeetathyon-es*	There aren't any rooms
No queda sitio *no keda seetyo*	There is no room
No hay plazas libres *no I plathas leebres*	There are no places
¿Para cuántas noches? *para kwantas noches?*	For how many nights?
¿Cuánto tiempo va a quedarse? *kwanto tee-yempo ba a kedarseh?*	How long are you staying?
¿Para cuántas personas? *para kwantas pairsonas?*	For how many people?
Está todo incluído *esta todo inklooeedo*	Everything is included
Firme aquí, por favor *feermeh akee por fabbor*	Sign here, please
¿Puede rellenar esta ficha? *pwedeh reh-yen-ar esta feecha?*	Could you fill in this form?
¿Me deja su pasaporte, por favor? *meh deh-ha soo pasaporteh, por fabbor?*	Could you give me your passport please?
No puedo ir (hoy) *no pwedo eer (oy)*	I can't go (today)
No puedo repararlo *no pwedo repararlo*	I can't repair it

- For other expressions of time, see page 133.

EATING OUT

- Eating and drinking in bars and restaurants is very much an integral part of Spanish everyday life. Children are welcome.
- Bars and cafeterias are open for most of the day until late at night. Restaurants generally serve meals between one o'clock and three o'clock for lunch and from about 9 o'clock until 11 o'clock for the evening meal. Times vary, and in most tourist areas restaurants are open longer. If you are unable to find a meal in a restaurant because of the time, there are usually plenty of bars available for food.
- Generally the service in Spanish restaurants and bars is very efficient and the food of good quality. Prices must be displayed by law. Look for the *Menú del Día* sign for the most economical meal. Restaurants are categorised by a fork symbol, from one to five forks, and cafeterias by a cup symbol. Expect to pay corresponding prices in top restaurants and cafeterias.

- It is customary practice to include a small tip (between 5% and 10%) in most bars and restaurants even though most bills carry the sign *Servicio Incluido* (service charge included). You will also see *IVA Incluido* on your bill. This is the equivalent of VAT.

- In most Spanish bars it is customary to pay one's bill as you leave. Prices vary depending on whether you stand at the bar or sit at a table. It is not customary to sit at a table already partially occupied by customers.

- In some large modern bars (in airports or department stores) you are given a form as you enter. The waiter will complete this for you and you pay the cashier as you leave.

- Spaniards usually eat the vegetable and meat courses separately. *Platos combinados* combine them in one course, as the British do.

- If you are not satisfied with service or food ask for the *Hoja de Reclamaciones* (the complaints book) which all bars and restaurants are obliged to carry.

You may see:

bar	bar
restaurante	restaurant
cafetería	luxury café also serving alcohol
cervecería	beer cellar
hamburguesería	hamburger/fast food bar
autoservicio	self-service
tapas	bar snacks
meriendas	afternoon snacks
desayunos	breakfasts
comidas	meals
buffet libre	self-service buffet
menú del día	menu of the day

At the bar

Waiter!	¡Camarero! *kamarerro!*
Waitress!	¡Camarera! *kamarerra!*
Excuse me, please	Oiga, por favor *oyga, por fabbor*
a cup/a mug of	una taza de *oona tatha deh*
a glass of	un vaso de *oon basso deh*
a bottle of	una botella de *oona botelya deh*
a jug of	una jarra de *oona harra deh*
half a bottle	media botella *medya botelya*
a can/a tin	una lata *oona latta*

Non alcoholic drinks

I'd like . . .	Quiero . . . *kee-yerro . . .*
. . . a black coffee	. . . un café solo *oon kafeh solo*
. . . a white coffee	. . . un café con leche *oon kafeh kon lecheh*
. . . a decaffeinated coffee (with milk)	. . . un descafeinado (con leche) *oon deskafeynado (kon lecheh)*
. . . a tea (with milk/lemon)	. . . un té (con leche/limón) *oon teh (kon lecheh/leemon)*

35

. . . a glass of milk	. . . un vaso de leche *oon basso deh lecheh*
. . . a (strawberry) milk shake	. . . un batido (de fresa) *oon bateedo (deh frehsa)*
. . . a carbonated/natural mineral water	. . . un agua mineral con gas/ sin gas *oon agwa meeneral kon gas/seen gas*
. . . a coca cola	. . . una coca cola *oona koka kola*
. . . a lemon drink	. . . una limonada *oona leemonada*
. . . an orange drink	. . . una naranjada *oona naranhada*
. . . a lemonade	. . . una gaseosa *oona gas-yosa*
. . . a tonic	. . . una tónica *oona tonnika*
a/an . . . juice	un zumo de . . . *oon thoomo deh . . .*
. . . apple	. . . manzana *manthana*
. . . grapefruit	. . . pomelo *pomelo*
. . . orange	. . . naranja *naranha*
. . . pineapple	. . . piña *peenya*
. . . tomato	. . . tomate *tomateh*
with cold milk	con leche fría *kon lecheh freea*
with hot milk	con leche caliente *kon lecheh kal-yenteh*

Alcoholic drinks

Could you give me . . .	Póngame . . . *pongameh . . .*
. . . a beer	. . . una cerveza *oona thairbetha*
. . . a cider	. . . una sidra *oona seedra*
. . . a red wine	. . . un vino tinto *oon beeno teento*
. . . a white wine	. . . un vino blanco *oon beeno blanko*
. . . a rosé wine	. . . un vino rosada *oon beeno rosado*
. . . a house wine	. . . un vino de la casa *oon beeno deh la kassa*
. . . a sherry	. . . un Jerez *oon hereth*
. . . (a glass of) champagne	. . . (una copa de) champán/ cava *(oona kopa deh) champan/kaba*
. . . a brandy/cognac	. . . un coñac *oon konyak*
. . . a gin	. . . una ginebra *oona heenebra*
. . . a gin and tonic	. . . un gin tonic *oon jeentoneek*
. . . a rum	. . . un ron *oon ron*
. . . a rum and coke	. . . un Cuba libre/un cubata *oon kooba leebreh/oon koobata*
. . . a (Scotch) whisky	. . . un whisky (escocés) *oon weeskee (eskothes)*

with ice	con hielo *kon yelo*
with water	con agua *kon agwa*
with soda	con soda *kon soda*
neat/on its own	solo/a *solo/a*
sweet	dulce *dooltheh*
dry	seco *sekko*

Try these special drinks

Non alcoholic

un café largo *oon kafeh largo*	a weak coffee with lots of water
un cortado *oon kortado*	a coffee with a drop of milk
un café con hielo *oon kafeh kon yelo*	coffee with ice
un chocolate (con churros) *oon chokolateh kon chooros)*	hot, thick chocolate (with fritters)
una horchata *oona orchata*	a drink made of nuts

Alcoholic

sangría *sangreea*	a drink made with wine, lemon and fruit
vino de Málaga *beeno deh malaga*	sweet wine
un moscatel *oon moskatel*	a sweet wine served with desserts and sweets or biscuits

Snacks

A . . . sandwich/roll, please	un sandwich/bocadillo . . . por favor *oon sandwich/bokadee-yo . . . por fabbor*
. . . cheese	. . . de queso *deh kesso*
. . . ham	. . . de jamón *deh hamon*
. . . toasted	. . . tostado *tostado*
. . . salami	. . . salchichón *salcheechon*
. . . spicy sausage	. . . chorizo *choreetho*
a hamburger	una hamburguesa *oona amboorgessa*
a portion/two portions of . . .	una ración de/dos raciones de . . . *oona rath-yon deh/dos rath-yones deh. . .*
olives	olivas *oleebas*
squid	calamares *kalamares*

Try these specialities

ensaladilla rusa *ensaladeeya roosa*	Russian salad, made with potatoes, vegetables and mayonnaise sauce
gambas (al ajillo) *gambas (al aheeyo)*	prawns (in garlic sauce)
jamón serrano *hamon seranno*	smoked ham

Restaurant

I'd like to reserve a table for . . .	Quiero reservar una mesa para . . . *kee-yerro resairbar oona messa para . . .*
. . . two	. . . dos *dos*
. . . eight o'clock	. . . las ocho *las ocho*
. . . tonight	. . . esta noche *esta nocheh*
. . . tomorrow	. . . mañana *man-yana*
I've reserved a table in the name of . . .	He reservado una mesa a nombre de . . . *eh resairbado oona messa a nombreh deh . . .*
I prefer that table	Prefiero aquella mesa *pref-yerro akel-ya messa*
Are there any free tables?	¿Hay mesas libres? *I messas leebres?*
There are five of us	Somos cinco *somos theenko*

You may hear:

No hay mesas libres *no I messas leebres*	There are no free tables
¿Para cuántas personas? *para kwantas pairsonas?*	For how many people?
Tendrán que esperar *tendran keh esperar*	You will have to wait
Pasen por aquí *passen por akee*	Could you come this way?

40

Eating Out

I'd like ...	Quiero ... *kee-yerro ...*
... the menu of the day	... el menú del día *el menoo del deea*
... the tourist menu	... el menú turístico *el menoo tooreesteeko*
... the menu	... la carta *la karta*
... the buffet	... el buffet libre *el boofeh leebreh*
... a typical, local dish	... un plato típico de aquí *oon platto teepeeko deh akee*
... something vegetarian	... algo vegetariano *algo beh-hetareeano*
... the wine list	... la lista de vinos *la leesta deh beenos*

What do you recommend?	¿Qué me recomienda? *keh meh rekom-yenda?*
What is this?	¿Qué es esto? *keh es esto?*
Has this got fish/meat?	¿Tiene esto pescado/carne? *tee-yenneh esto peskado/karneh?*

You may hear:

Le recomiendo ... *leh rekom-yendo ...*	I recommend ...
No nos queda *no nos keda*	We haven't got any left
En seguida se lo cambio *en segeeda seh lo kamb-yo*	I'll change it immediately

Could you bring . . . ?	¿Puede traer . . . ? *pwedeh tryair . . . ?*
. . . some bread	. . . pan *pan*
. . . pepper	. . . pimienta *pim-yenta*
. . . salt	. . . sal *sal*
. . . sugar	. . . azúcar *athookar*
. . . water	. . . agua *agwa*
. . . a fork	. . . un tenedor *oon tenedor*
. . . a glass	. . . un vaso *oon basso*
. . . a knife	. . . un cuchillo *oon koochee-yo*
. . . a serviette	. . . una servilleta *oona sairbee-yetta*
. . . a spoon	. . . una cuchara *oona koochara*

You may hear:

¿Qué tomará/tomarán de primero/de segundo (plato)? *keh tomara/tomaran deh preemero/deh segoondo (plato)?*	What will you have for the first/second course?
¿Quiere algo de postre? *kee-yerreh algo deh postreh?*	Would you like something for dessert?
¿Para beber? *para bebair*	To drink?
¿Le/les gusta? *leh/les goosta?*	Do you like it?

Ordering

For the first course I'd like . . .	De primer plato quiero . . . *deh preemair platto kee-yerro . . .*
. . . mixed salad	. . . ensalada mixta *ensalada meexta*
. . . plain omelette	. . . tortilla francesa *tortee-ya franthessa*
. . . fish soup	. . . sopa de pescado *sopa deh peskado*

● For others see page 45.

For the main course, . . .	De segundo plato . . . *deh segoondo plato . . .*
. . . (lamb) chops	. . . chuletas (de cordero) *choolettas (deh kordero)*
. . . roast chicken	. . . pollo asado *poyo asado*
. . . steak and chips	. . . filete con patatas fritas *feeleteh kon patatas freetas*

● For others see page 46.

For sweet . . .	De postre . . . *deh postreh . . .*
. . . fresh fruit	. . . fruta del tiempo *froota del tee-yempo*
. . . cream caramel	. . . flan *flan*
. . . ice cream dessert	. . . tarta helada *tarta elada*

● For others see page 46.

You may see:

especialidad de la casa	house speciality
primer plato	starter (first dish)
segundo plato	main dish
postre	sweet/dessert
bebidas	drinks
plato del día	dish of the day
platos combinados	complete meals on a plate
menú a la carta	menu 'à la carte'
menú del día	menu of the day
menú turístico	tourist menu
buffet libre	buffet
lista de vinos	wine list
entradas	starters
entremeses	starters/hors d'oeuvres
ensaladas	salads
sopas	soups
huevos	eggs
tortillas	omelettes
verduras	greens
pescados	fish
mariscos	sea food
carnes	meat
quesos	cheeses
pastelería	cakes/sweets
helados	ice-cream
frutas	fruit
cubierto	cover charge
servicio incluído	service included

Eating Out

Primer plato	First course
arroz a la cubana *aroth a la koobana*	rice with fried eggs, fried bananas in tomato sauce
caldo *kaldo*	meat and vegetable broth
cocido (madrileño) *kotheedo (madreelenyo)*	a stew made of chick peas and meat
consomé (con yema/al Jerez) *konsomeh (kon yema/al hereth)*	chicken broth (with egg yoke/ with sherry)
gazpacho *gathpacho*	a cold vegetable soup made with tomatoes, cucumber, peppers, onion and garlic
huevos al plato *webbos al platto*	fried eggs
menestra de verduras *menestra deh bairdooras*	mixed fried vegetables with ham
paella de mariscos *py-eya deh mareeskos*	sea-food paella
paella valenciana *py-eya balenthee-yana*	paella made with chicken, sea-food and vegetables.
pescaditos fritos *peskadeetos freetos*	fried small fish
pulpo (a la gallega) *poolpo (a la ga-yega)*	octopus (with sweet chilli and olive oil)
tortilla de patata *tortee-ya deh patata*	Spanish omelette (made with potatoes and onion)
una empanadilla *oona empanadee-ya*	a savoury-filled pastry
pimientos rellenos *peem-yentos reyenos*	stuffed peppers
albóndigas *albondeegas*	meat balls

Segundo plato	Second course
almejas a la marinera *almeh-has a la mareenera*	clams in white wine sauce
callos a la madrileña *ka-yos a la madreelenya*	tripe in piquant sauce
cochinillo asado *kocheenee-yo asado*	roast piglet
conejo (con alioli) *koneh-ho (kon aleeolee)*	rabbit (with garlic mayonnaise)
chuletas a la brasa *choolettas a la brassa*	barbecued chops
merluza a la vasca *mairlootha a la baska*	hake in béchamel and asparagus sauce
parrillada (de pescado y marisco) *paree-yada deh peskado ee mareesko*	mixed grill (fish and sea-food)
pollo a la chilindrón *poyo a la cheelleendron*	chicken fried with tomatoes, peppers, onion and ham
riñones al Jerez *reen-yones al hereth*	kidneys in sherry
trucha a la navarra/con jamón *troocha a la nabara/kon hamon*	trout filled with ham

Postre	Dessert
crema catalana *kremma katalana*	thick custard with burnt sugar on top
macedonia de frutas *mathedonya deh frootas*	fruit salad
melocotón con vino *melokoton kon beeno*	peaches marinated in wine
natillas *natee-yas*	custard
turrón *tooron*	nougat

Ways of cooking food

bien hecho *bee-yen echo*	well done
poco hecho *poko echo*	rare
caliente *kal-yenteh*	hot
frío *freeo*	cold
al ajillo *al ahee-yo*	with garlic
ahumado *aoomado*	smoked
asado *asado*	roast
cocido *kotheedo*	boiled
crudo *kroodo*	raw
duro *dooro*	hard boiled
en escabeche *en eskabecheh*	marinated/pickled
frito *freeto*	fried
con guarnición *con gwarneeth-yon*	accompanied by vegetables and/or chips
a la plancha *a la plancha*	grilled
relleno *reyeno*	stuffed/filled
del tiempo *del tee-yempo*	of the season

Problems

I didn't ask for that	Yo no he pedido eso *yo no eh pedeedo eso*
This isn't for me	Esto no es para mí *esto no es para mee*
Could you heat it a bit more?	¿Puede calentarlo un poco más? *pwedeh kalentarlo oon poko mas?*

It's a bit . . .	Está un poco . . . *esta oon poko . . .*
. . . cold	. . . frío *freeo*
. . . underdone	. . . crudo *kroodo*
. . . burnt	. . . quemado *kemado*

I don't think this is right	Creo que esto no está bien *kray-o keh esto no esta bee-yen*
This bill isn't mine/is wrong	Esta cuenta no es la mía/está equivocada *esta kwenta no es la meea/esta ekeebokada*
I didn't have that	No he tomado eso *no eh tomado eso*

You may hear:

Le traigo otro *leh trygo otro*	I'll bring you another
Se lo caliento *seh lo kal-yento*	I'll heat it up

ENTERTAINMENT
AND SPORT

- Smoking is not permitted in any part of Spanish cinemas.
- If you are shown to your seat by an usher (*acomodador/a*), a small tip is in order.
- Cinemas often open at 4 or 5 pm and show films every two hours, depending on the length of the film. Alternatively, they may advertise *Sesión Continua* (continuous performance). Check in the newspaper or on notice boards (*Cartelera*).
- In most towns, cinemas have reduced prices one day a week (*el día del espectador*), usually Monday or Wednesday.
- Most foreign films are dubbed into Spanish. Some are shown in their original version (*versión original – VO*) and subtitled (*subtitulado*).
- The authorities make recommendations as to the suitability of films to different age groups but cannot turn people away on the grounds of age. Look for the following:

recomendada a todos los públicos ('U' certificate)
recomendada a mayores de 18 años ('18' certificate)

- As well as getting you in to a discotheque, the entrance ticket is valid for one drink. Subsequent drinks can be rather expensive.
- Beware of 'invitations' (*invitaciones*) to discotheques handed out in many resorts. These get you in but they don't get you a drink, so you spend the same as with a normal entrance fee.

- The bullfighting season runs from March to October and one particular town will only have a small number of fights in one season. They usually take place on Sundays.
- Every town and village in Spain has its annual *fiesta* and it is during this that some form of bullfighting or bull running (through the streets) takes place. The most famous of these events takes place in Pamplona.

- Football is much more expensive than in Britain.
- Matches usually take place on Sundays during the late afternoon (4 pm onwards).
- Tickets are usually available at the gate unless it is an important match when the game is likely to be sold out in advance.

- Entrance to museums is not usually free, although students with an international student card are admitted free.
- Check opening times in the local press, as these vary. Many museums are closed on Mondays.

cinema	el cine *el theeneh*
theatre	el teatro *el tay-atro*
night club	el club *el kloob*
night club/dance hall	la sala de fiestas *la salla deh fee-yestas*

Entertainment and Sport

One ticket, please	Una entrada, por favor *oona entrada, por fabbor*
One child's ticket	Una entrada de niño *oona entrada deh neenyo*
I'd like to reserve 4 tickets	Quiero reservar 4 entradas *kee-yerro resairbar kwatro entradas*
How much is it?	¿Cuánto es? *kwanto es?*
Do you have tickets for the 7 o'clock performance?	¿Hay entradas para las siete? *I entradas para las see-yetteh?*

Is there a discount . . . ?	¿Hay descuento . . . ? *I deskwento . . . ?*
. . . today	. . . hoy *oy*
. . . for students	. . . para estudiantes *para estood-yantes*
. . . for pensioners	. . . para pensionistas *para pens-yoneestas*
. . . for children	. . . para los niños *para los neenyos*

When does . . . open?	¿Cuándo abre . . . ? *kwando abreh . . . ?*
When does . . . close?	¿Cuándo cierra . . . ? *kwando thee-yera . . . ?*
. . . the discotheque	. . . la discoteca *la deeskoteka*
. . . the sports complex	. . . el polideportivo *el poleedeporteevo*

At the cinema and theatre

What time is . . . ?	¿A qué hora es . . . ? *a keh ora es . . . ?*
. . . the (afternoon) showing	. . . la sesión (de tarde) *la ses-yon (deh tardeh)*
. . . the film	. . . la película *la peleekoola*
. . . the play	. . . la obra *la obra*
. . . the (evening) performance/show	. . . la función (de noche) *la funkth-yon (deh nocheh)*
. . . the concert	. . . el concierto *el konth-yairto*
. . . the opera	. . . la ópera *la opera*
I'd like . . .	Quiero . . . *kee-yerro*
. . . stalls (orchestra)	. . . butaca *bootakka*
. . . circle (mezzanine)	. . . anfiteatro *anfeetay-atro*
. . . pit/orchestra	. . . platea *plateh-a*
. . . a (500) peseta ticket	. . . una entrada de (500) pesetas *oona entrada deh (keenyentas) pesetas*
Are they numbered?	¿Son numeradas? *son noomeradas?*
Is it a continuous showing?	¿Es sesión continua? *es ses-yon konteenwa?*

at the front/back	delante/detrás *delanteh/detras*
in the middle	en el medio *en el med-yo*
I want a programme, please	Un programa, por favor *oon programa, por fabbor*

Discotheques and nightclubs

Is there . . . ?	¿Hay . . . ? *I . . . ?*
. . . a show	. . . espectáculo *espektakoolo*
. . . a music group	. . . algún grupo musical *algoon groopo mooseekal*
Is there a drink included?	¿Está incluida la consumición? *esta inklooeeda la konsoomeeth-yon?*
I have this invitation	Tengo esta invitación *tengo esta inbeetath-yon*
Do you have to wear evening dress?	¿Hay que ir con traje de noche/de etiqueta? *I keh eer kon traheh deh nocheh/deh eteeketa?*

Other useful expressions

Where is the cloakroom?	¿Dónde está el guardarropa? *dondeh esta el gwardaropa?*
Where are the toilets?	¿Dónde están los servicios? *dondeh estan los sairbeeth-yos?*
I'd like to cancel a reservation	Quiero cancelar una reserva *kee-yerro kanthelar oona resairba*

At a bullfight

Where is the bull ring?	¿Dónde está la plaza de toros? *dondeh esta la platha deh toros?*
When is the bull fight?	¿Cuándo es la corrida? *kwando es la koreeda?*
A ticket . . .	Una entrada . . . *oona entrada . . .*
. . . in the shade	. . . de sombra *deh sombra*
. . . in the sun	. . . de sol *deh sol*
. . . in a good place	. . . en un buen sitio *en oon bwen seet-yo*
I'd like a cushion, please	Quiero una almohadilla, por favor *kee-yerro oona almoadee-ya, por fabbor*
How long does the bullfight last?	¿Cuánto tiempo dura la corrida? *kwanto tee-yempo doora la koreeda?*

You may hear:

No hay entradas *no I entradas*	We have no tickets left
Es gratis *es gratees*	It's free
No hacemos reservas *no athemos resairbas*	We don't take reservations
No tenemos venta anticipada *no tenemos benta anteetheepada*	We don't have advance sales

Sports

A ticket ...	Una entrada ... *oona entrada ...*
... for a seat	... sentado *sentado*
... for standing	... de pie *deh pee-yeh*
... in the stand	... de tribuna *deh treeboona*
... on the terrace	... de general *deh heneral*
What time is the match?	¿A qué hora es el partido? *a keh ora es el parteedo?*
Can one ... here?	¿Se puede ... aquí? *seh pwedeh ... akee?*
... dive	... bucear *bootheh-ar*
... fish	... pescar *peskar*
... go horse riding	... montar a caballo *montar a kaba-yo*
... go sailing	... navegar *nabegar*
... play tennis	... jugar al tenis *hoogar al tenees*
... ride a bicycle	... ir en bicicleta *eer en beetheekletta*
... swim	... nadar *naddar*
... water-ski	... hacer esquí acuático *athair eskee akwateeko*

Is there . . . here/near here?	¿Hay . . . aquí/cerca? *I . . . akee/thairka?*
. . . a golf course	. . . un campo de golf *oon kampo deh golf*
. . . an (indoor) swimming pool	. . . una piscina (cubierta) *oona pistheena (koobyairta)*
. . . a sports centre	. . . un polideportivo *oon poleedeporteebo*
. . . a tennis court	. . . una pista de tenis *oona peesta deh tenees*

Can I hire . . . ?	¿Puedo alquilar . . . ? *pwedo alkeelar . . . ?*
. . . a bicycle	. . . una bicicleta *oona beetheekletta*
. . . a (small) boat	. . . una barca *oona barka*
. . . a deck chair/a sun bed	. . . una hamaca *oona amaka*
. . . a pedal boat	. . . un patín *oon pateen*
. . . some skis	. . . unos esquís *oonos eskees*
. . . some ski boots	. . . unas botas de esquí *oonas botas deh eskee*
. . . a tennis racket	. . . una raqueta de tenis *oona raketta deh tenees*
. . . a windsurf board	. . . una tabla de windsurf *oona tabla deh weendsoorf*
. . . all the equipment	. . . todo el equipo *todo el ekeepo*

Do you have to pay to get in/become a member?	¿Hay que pagar para entrar/hacerse socio? *I keh pagar para entrar/athairseh soth-yo*
I would like . . . lessons	Quiero clases de . . . *kee-yerro klasses deh . . .*
. . . tennis	. . . tenis *tenees*
. . . ski	. . . esquí *eskee*
How much is it per hour/per day?	¿Cuánto es por hora/por día? *kwanto es por ora/por deea?*
Is there a lifeguard/a Red Cross post?	¿Hay socorrista/un puesto de Cruz Roja? *I sokoreesta/oon pwesto deh krooth roha?*

Visiting the town

Where is/are . . . ?	¿Dónde está/están . . . ? *dondeh esta/estan . . . ?*
. . . the castle	. . . el castillo *el kastee-yo*
. . . the cathedral	. . . la catedral *la katedral*
. . . the (open air) market	. . . el mercado (al aire libre) *el mairkado (al ayreh leebreh)*
. . . the museum	. . . el museo *el mooseyo*
. . . the (main) square	. . . la plaza (Mayor) *la platha (my-or)*
. . . the ruins	. . . las ruinas *las rooeenas*
. . . the shops	. . . las tiendas *las tee-yendas*

When do they open/close?	¿Cuándo abren/cierran? *kwando abren/thee-yeran?*
Is it open (on Sundays)?	¿Está abierto (los domingos)? *esta ab-yairto (los domeengos)?*
Can I take photos?	¿Se puede hacer fotos? *seh pwedeh athair fotos?*
Do you have postcards?	¿Tiene postales? *tee-yenneh postales?*
Can you recommend an excursion?	¿Puede recomendarme una excursión? *pwedeh rekomendarmeh oona exkoors-yon?*
How long does it last?	¿Cuánto dura? *kwanto doora?*

● For directions and other enquiries, see page 10.

You may hear:

Tiene que dejar . . . aquí *tee-yenneh keh de-har . . . akee*	You have to leave . . . here
. . . su bolso *soo bolso*	. . . your bag
. . . su abrigo *soo abreego*	. . . your coat
. . . su paraguas *soo paragwas*	. . . your umbrella
No está permitido hacer fotos *no esta pairmeeteedo athair fotos*	It's not permitted/allowed to take pictures
Hay que ser socio *I keh sair soth-yo*	You have to be a member

Meeting people

- When meeting people, or saying goodbye, it is usual to shake hands.
- Members of the family and close friends often kiss each other on each cheek on meeting and saying goodbye.
- Spaniards use 'Please' (*por favor*) and 'Thank you' (*gracias*) less than English speakers and tend to be more direct in their speech. This is not a sign of rudeness. The normal response to *gracias* is *de nada* ('Don't mention it').

Good morning	Buenos días *bwennos deeas*
Good afternoon/evening	Buenas tardes *bwennas tardes*
Good night	Buenas noches *bwennas noches*
Hallo!	¡Hola! *ola!*
How are you? (**formal**)	¿Cómo está usted? *komo esta oosted?*
How are you? (**informal**)	¿Qué tal (estás)? *keh tal (estas)?*
Very well, thanks	Muy bien, gracias *mwee bee-yen, grath-yas*
Alright	Bien *bee-yen*
Not bad	Regular *regoolar*
And you? (**formal**)	¿Y usted? *ee oosted?*
And you? (**informal**)	¿Y tú? *ee too?*
Is this seat occupied?	¿Está ocupada (esta silla)? *esta okoopada (esta see-ya)?*

Entertainment and Sport

You may hear:

Está ... *esta ...*	It's ...
... libre *leebreh*	... free
... ocupado *okoopado*	... occupied

I am/my name is ...	Me llamo ... *meh yamo ...*
What's your name? (formal)	¿Cómo se llama usted? *komo seh yama oosted?*
What's your name? (informal)	¿Cómo te llamas? *komo teh yamas?*
Pleased to meet you	Mucho gusto *moocho goosto*
One moment, please	Un momento, por favor *oon momento, por fabbor*
It doesn't matter	No importa *no eemporta*
I don't understand	No comprendo *no komprendo*
Could you ... ?	¿Puede ... ? *pwedeh ... ?*
... repeat that	... repetirlo *repeteerlo*
... speak more slowly	... hablar más despacio *ablar mas despath-yo*
... translate it into English	... traducirlo al inglés *tradootheerlo al in-gles*
I don't speak Spanish	No hablo español *no ablo espanyol*

I speak a little Spanish	Hablo un poco de español *ablo oon poko deh espanyol*
Do you speak English?	¿Habla inglés? *abla in-gles*
What is this called in Spanish?	¿Cómo se llama esto en español? *komo seh yama esto en espanyol?*

This is ...	Éste/ésta es ... *esteh/esta es ...*

... my husband	... mi marido *mee mareedo*
... my fiancé/boyfriend	... mi novio *mee nobyo*
... my friend (male)	... mi amigo *mee ameego*
... my son	... mi hijo *mee ee-ho*
... my wife	... mi esposa *mee esposa*
... my fiancée/girl friend	... mi novia *mee nobya*
... my friend (female)	... mi amiga *mee ameega*
... my daughter	... mi hija *mee ee-ha*

I'm ...	Soy ... *soy ...*

... American	... americano/a *amereekano/a*
... Australian	... australiano/a *owstral-yano/a*
... Canadian	... canadiense *kanad-yenseh*

61

... English	... inglés/inglesa
	in-gles/inglessa
... Irish	... irlandés/irlandesa
	eerlandes/eerlandessa
... Scottish	... escocés/escocesa
	eskothes/eskothessa
... Welsh	... galés/galesa
	gales/galessa

Are you (Spanish)? (formal)	¿Es usted (español/española)
	es oosted (espanyol/
	espanyola)?
Are you (South American)?	¿Eres (sudamericano/a)?
(informal)	*e-res (soodamereekano/a)?*
Where do you come from?	¿De dónde eres?
	deh dondeh e-res?
I live ...	Vivo ...
	beebo ...
... in London	... en Londres
	en londres
... in New York	... en Nueva York
	en nweba york
... in the north of England	... en el norte de Inglaterra
	en el norteh deh inglaterr
I have ...	Tengo ...
	tengo ...
... a son/a daughter	... un hijo/una hija
	oon ee-ho/oona ee-ha
... two children	... dos hijos
	dos ee-hos
I don't have any children	No tengo hijos
	no tengo ee-hos
I'm on holiday	Estoy de vacaciones
	estoy deh bakath-yones

I work here	Trabajo aquí *traba-ho akee*
I'm a student	Soy estudiante *soy estood-yanteh*
And you? (formal)	¿Y usted? *ee oosted?*
And you? (informal)	¿Y tú? *ee too?*

Would you like to . . . ?	¿Quieres . . . ? *kee-yerres . . . ?*
. . dance	. . . bailar *bylar*
. . have something to drink/ eat	. . . tomar algo *tomar algo*
. . come out with me (tomorrow)	. . . salir conmigo (mañana) *saleer konmeego (man- yana)*
. . go out for dinner/supper	. . . ir a comer/cenar *eer a komair/thennar*

I'll treat you	Te invito *teh eenbeeto*
Where shall we meet?	¿Dónde quedamos? *dondeh kedamos?*
Can I call you/pick you up?	¿Puedo llamarte/ir a buscarte? *pwedo yamarteh/eer a booskarteh?*
No thanks	No gracias *no grath-yas*
I can't	No puedo *no pwedo*

Goodbye	Adiós *ad-yos*
See you later	Hasta luego *asta lwego*
See you soon	Hasta pronto *asta pronto*

Business expressions

I'm ...	Soy ... *soy ...*
... Mr (Smith)	... el señor (Smith) *el senyor (smeeth)*
... Mrs (Smith)	... la señora (Smith) *la senyora (smeeth)*
... Miss (Smith)	... la señorita (Smith) *la senyoreeta (smeeth)*
I'm from the ... Company	Soy de la Compañía ... *soy deh la kompan-yeea ...*
I have an appointment with ...	Tengo una cita con ... *tengo oona theeta kon ...*
Could I ... ?	¿Podría ... ? *podreea ... ?*
... see Mr (Pérez)	... ver al señor (Pérez) *bair al senyor (pereth)*
... speak to Miss (Pérez)	... hablar con la señorita (Pérez) *ablar kon la senyoreeta (pereth)*
Here is my card	Aquí tiene mi tarjeta *akee tee-yenneh mee tarhetta*
I'm sorry I'm late	Siento llegar tarde *see-yento yegar tardeh*
I'm in the hotel (Goya)	Estoy en el hotel (Goya) *estoy en el otel (goya)*

● For other business expressions see page 118.

HEALTH

- In Spain you can obtain free medical attention providing you take with you proof of your National Insurance contributions (eg your National Insurance card or a pay slip).
- Dentists are very expensive and only provide limited services within the National Health Service.
- In case of accident or emergency go to an emergency first aid centre (*Casa de Socorro*) or the nearest hospital (*hospital*) and look for the sign *urgencias*.
- If you require treatment on the road, there are first aid posts (*puesto de socorro de Cruz Roja*) at regular intervals.
- If you need a doctor look for:
  médico (doctor)
  consultorio (doctor's surgery)
  ambulatorio (health centre).
- If you need an ambulance look for: *ambulancia*.
- If you need an injection the doctor will refer you to a *practicante*.

- Medicines can be obtained from chemists (*farmacia*). You have to pay a percentage of the prescription unless you are a pensioner. Outside each chemist there is a list of local chemists which are open 24 hours a day (*farmacia de guardia*).
- Chemists are identified by a red or green cross symbol.

Asking for help

Can you help me, please?	Ayúdeme, por favor *ayoodehmeh, por fabbor*
I don't speak Spanish	No hablo español *no ablo espanyol*
Do you speak English?	¿Habla inglés? *abla in-gles?*

I need . . .	Necesito . . . *netheseeto . . .*
. . . a doctor	. . . un médico *oon mediko*
. . . an interpreter	. . . un intérprete *oon eentairpreteh*
. . . to go to hospital	. . . ir al hospital *eer al ospeetal*

Where is . . . ?	¿Dónde está . . . ? *dondeh esta . . . ?*
. . . the hospital	. . . el hospital *el ospeetal*
. . . the doctor's surgery	. . . la consulta (del doctor) *la konsoolta (del doktor)*
. . . the 'emergencies' entrance	. . . la entrada de urgencias *la entrada deh oorhenth-yas*

It's urgent/serious	Es urgente/grave *es oorhenteh/grabeh*
I am ill/injured	Estoy enfermo/herido/a *estoy enfairmo/ereedo/a*
I've had an accident	He tenido un accidente *eh teneedo oon aktheedenteh*
Can you call an ambulance/ take me to hospital?	¿Puede llamar a una ambulancia/llevarme al hospital? *pwedeh yamar a oona amboolanth-ya/yebbarmeh al ospeetal?*
Is there a doctor . . . ?	¿Hay un médico . . . ? *I oon mediko . . . ?*
. . . here	. . . aquí *akee*
. . . in the hotel	. . . en el hotel *en el otel*
. . . in the campsite	. . . en el camping *en el kampeeng*
Is there a nurse/a first-aid box?	Hay enfermera/botiquín? *I enfairmera/boteekeen*
Can the doctor come . . . ?	¿Puede venir el doctor . . . ? *pwedeh beneer el doktor . . . ?*
. . . now	. . . ahora *a-ora*
. . . today	. . . hoy *oy*
. . . as soon as possible	. . . cuanto antes *kwanto antes*
My address is . . .	Mi dirección es . . . *mee deerekth-yon es . . .*

At the doctor's

What time is the surgery open?	¿A qué hora es la visita? *a keh ora es la biseeta?*
Could you give me an appointment with . . . ?	¿Me da hora para . . . ? *meh da ora para . . . ?*
. . . the doctor (GP)	. . . el médico (de cabecera) *el mediko (deh kabetherra)*
. . . eye specialist	. . . el oculista *el okooleesta*
. . . the gynaecologist	. . . el ginecólogo *el heenehkologo*
. . . the dentist	. . . el dentista *el denteesta*
. . . the specialist	. . . el especialista *el espeth-yaleesta*
It hurts me here	Me duele aquí *meh dwelleh akee*
My . . . hurts	Me duele . . . *meh dwelleh . . .*
My . . . hurt	Me duelen . . . *meh dwellen . . .*
. . . ankle	. . . el tobillo *el tobee-yo*
. . . arm	. . . el brazo *el bratho*
. . . back	. . . la espalda *la espalda*
. . . breast/chest	. . . el pecho *el pecho*
. . . ear	. . . el oído *el oyeedo*

... eye	... el ojo *el oho*
... finger	... el dedo *el dedo*
... foot	... el pie *el pee-yeh*
... hand	... la mano *la mano*
... head	... la cabeza *la kabetha*
... knee	... la rodilla *la rodee-ya*
... leg	... la pierna *la pee-yairna*
... lung	... el pulmón *el poolmon*
... mouth	... la boca *la boka*
... neck	... el cuello *el kweyo*
... penis	... el pene *el peneh*
... shoulder	... el hombro *el ombro*
... stomach	... el estómago *el estomago*
... throat	... la garganta *la garganta*
... vagina	... la vagina *la baheena*
... wrist	... la muñeca *la moon-yekka*
... joints	... las articulaciones *las arteekoolath-yones*

It hurts . . .	Me duele . . .
	meh dwelleh . . .
. . . a lot	. . . mucho
	moocho
. . . a little	. . . un poco
	oon poko
. . . all the time	. . . continuamente
	konteenwamenteh
. . . sometimes	. . . a veces
	a beth-es

It's been hurting . . .	Me duele . . .
	meh dwelleh . . .
. . . since yesterday	. . . desde ayer
	desdeh ayair
. . . for two days	. . . desde hace dos días
	desdeh atheh dos deeas
. . . for a few hours	. . . desde hace unas horas
	desdeh atheh oonas oras
It's a sharp pain	Es un dolor agudo
	es oon dolor agoodo
I feel . . .	Estoy . . .
	estoy . . .
. . . faint	. . . mareado/a
	mareyado/a
. . . weak	. . . débil
	debeel
. . . worse	. . . peor
	peyor
I am constipated	Estoy estreñido/a
	estoy estren-yeedo/a
I have a cold	Estoy resfriado/a
	estoy resfreeado

have . . .	Tengo . . .
	tengo . . .

. . cramps	. . . calambres
	kalambres

. . diarrhoea	. . . diarrea
	deearea

. . insomnia	. . . insomnio
	eensomnyo

. . a migraine	. . . jaqueca
	hakekka

. . a rash	. . . un sarpullido
	oon sarpoo-yeedo

. . a stiff neck	. . . tortícolis
	torteekolees

think I have . . .	Creo que tengo . . .
	kray-o keh tengo . . .

. . broken something	. . . una fractura
	oona fraktoora

. . the flu	. . . la gripe
	la greepeh

. . food poisoning	. . . una intoxicación
	oona eentoxeekath-yon

. . indigestion	. . . una indigestión
	oona eendee-hest-yon

. . an infection	. . . una infección
	oona eenfekth-yon

. . sinusitis	. . . sinusitis
	seenooseetees

. . sun stroke	. . . una insolación
	oona eensolath-yon

. . a temperature	. . . fiebre
	fee-yebbreh

It itches	Me pica *meh peeka*
I can't breathe properly/move (my arm)/walk	No puedo respirar bien/mover (el brazo)/andar *no pwedo respeerar bee-yen/mobair (el bratho)/andar*
It's infected/swollen	Está infectado/a/inflamado/a *esta eenfektado/a/eenflamado/a*

What's happened?

I've fallen over	Me he caído *meh eh ka-yeedo*
I've burned myself	Me he quemado *meh eh kemado*
I've cut myself	Me he cortado *meh eh kortado*
I've bumped myself	Me he dado un golpe *meh eh dado oon golpeh*
I've taken this	He tomado esto *eh tomado esto*

My friend . . .	Mi amigo/a . . . *mee ameego/a . . .*
. . . is injured	. . . está herido/a *esta ereedo/a*
. . . is ill	. . . está enfermo/a *esta enfairmo*
. . . is unconscious	. . . está inconsciente *esta eenkonsth-yenteh*
. . . has fainted	. . . se ha desmayado *seh a desmayado*
. . . has had a (heart) attack	. . . ha tenido un ataque (al corazón) *a teneedo oon atakeh (al korathon)*

I've been stung/bitten by ...	Me ha picado/mordido ... *meh a peekado/mordeedo ...*
... something	... algo *algo*
... an insect	... un insecto *oon eensekto*
... a mosquito	... un mosquito *oon moskeeto*
... a wasp	... una avispa *oona abeespa*
... a bee	... una abeja *oona abeh-ha*
... a dog	... un perro *oon perro*
... a snake	... una serpiente *oona sairp-yenteh*

General conditions

I have ...	Tengo ... *tengo ...*
... asthma	... asma *asma*
... diabetes	... diabetes *deeabetes*
... high/low blood pressure	... la tensión alta/baja *la tens-yon alta/baha*
I'm allergic to penicillin/antibiotics	Tengo alergia a la penicilina/los antibióticos *tengo alairheea a la peneetheeleena/los anteebeeoteekos*
I take the Pill/this medicine	Tomo la píldora/esta medicina *tomo la peeldora/esta medeetheena*

73

I'm (3 months) pregnant	Estoy embarazada (de tres meses) *estoy embarathada (deh tres meses)*
I have a heart condition	Estoy enfermo/a del corazón *estoy enfairmo/a del korathon*
I had a heart attack	Tuve un infarto *toobeh oon eenfarto*

Questions

Could you give me something . . . ?	¿Puede darme algo . . . ? *pwedeh darmeh algo . . . ?*
. . . for the pain	. . . para el dolor *para el dolor*
. . . to sleep	. . . para dormir *para dormeer*
I (don't) want . . .	(No) quiero . . . *(no) kee-yerro . . .*
. . . injections	. . . inyecciones *eenyekth-yones*
. . . suppositories	. . . supositorios *sooposeetor-yos*
When do I have to take it?	¿Cuándo tengo que tomarlo? *kwando tengo keh tomarlo?*
Do I have to stay in bed?	¿Tengo que guardar cama? *tengo keh gwardar kama?*

When can I . . . ?	¿Cuándo puedo . . . ? *kwando pwedo . . . ?*
. . . sunbathe	. . . tomar el sol *tomar el sol*
. . . bathe	. . . bañarme *banyarmeh*

At the optician's

Can you repair my glasses?	¿Puede arreglar mis gafas? *pwedeh areglar mees gafas?*
I've lost my contact lenses	He perdido mis lentes de contacto *eh pairdeedo mees lentes deh kontakto*
I have something in this eye	Tengo algo en este ojo *tengo algo en esteh oho*

At the dentist

It aches here	Me duele aquí *meh dwelleh akee*
This tooth/this molar/my gum aches	Este diente/esta muela/la encía me duele *esteh dee-yenteh/esta mwella/ la entheea meh dwelleh*
A filling has fallen out	Se me ha caído un empaste *seh meh a ka-yeedo oon empasteh*
I have an abscess	Tengo un flemón *tengo oon flemon*
Please don't take out my tooth	No me saque la muela, por favor *no meh sakeh la mwella, por fabbor*
Can you fix my dentures?	¿Puede arreglar la dentadura? *pwedeh areglar la dentadoora?*

Paying

How much do I owe you?	¿Cuánto le debo? *kwanto leh debbo?*
Do I have to pay something now?	¿Tengo que pagar algo ahora? *tengo keh pagar algo a-ora?*

I have this insurance	Tengo este seguro *tengo esteh segooro*
Could you . . . ?	¿Puede . . . ? *pwedeh . . . ?*
. . . give me a receipt	. . . darme un recibo *darmeh oon retheebo*
. . . give me a medical certificate	. . . darme un certificado médico *darmeh oon thairteefeekado mediko*
. . . fill this in	. . . rellenar esto *reyenar esto*

You may hear:

¿Dónde le duele? *dondeh leh dwelleh?*	Where does it hurt?
Tome esto *tomeh esto*	Take this
cada (cuatro) horas *kada (kwatro) oras*	every (four) hours
antes/después de las comidas *antes/despwes deh las komeedas*	before/after meals
(tres) veces al día *(tres) bethes al deea*	(three) times a day
Guarde cama *gwardeh kama*	Stay in bed
No se bañe *no seh banyeh*	Don't bathe
Tiene que ir al hospital *tee-yeneh keh eer al ospeetal*	You have to go to the hospital
Vuelva mañana *bwelba man-yana*	Come back tomorrow

TRAVEL

By train

The Spanish national railway network is known as
RENFE (*Red Nacional de Ferrocarriles Españoles*). It
operates a number of different kinds of trains, usually
for different types of journeys. The main ones are as
follows:

- **Talgo**: a fast, luxury, inter-city train
- **TER**: a fast inter-city train
- **Rápido**: a long-distance stopping train with
  compartments
- **Electrotrén**: similar to the *Rápido* but more
  modern and with open-plan carriages
- **Expreso**: the night-train equivalent to the *Rápido*
- **Tranvía/Omnibus/Automotor**: local, stopping
  trains.

When buying a ticket for a long journey it is
advisable to make a seat reservation at least twenty-
four hours before your journey. If you are too late to

77

reserve a seat, ask the ticket collector (*revisor*) to help you find an unreserved seat.
- Look out for discount offers, especially '*Días Azules*' (Blue Days) when you can travel more cheaply. Ask for a calendar (*Calendario de días Azules*) at the information desk.
- Other discounts include *Chequetrén* (a type of travel card which offers 15% reductions), *Tarjeta joven* for young people, *Tarjeta turística* for tourists, and other family and group reductions. Ask at the information desk.
- Inter-rail cards are available in Britain if you are under twenty-six years of age.
- The main stations are now equipped with automatic ticket vending machines (*autoventa de billetes*), which issue tickets for long distance journeys and accept most major credit cards.
- Some long distance trains also offer nursery facilities (*coche guardería*) for young children from 2 to 11 years old.
- Spanish law requires that passengers under the age of sixteen may only travel alone if they carry a written authorisation from their parents or guardian.
- Children travel free up to the age of three and pay half price up to the age of seven.
- RENFE also puts on special 'scenic trains' for tourist (*trenes turísticos*).
- Further information can be obtained from the Spanish National Tourist Office (57/58 St James' Street, London SW1A 1LD).

Do you have . . . ?	¿Tienen . . . ? *tee-yennen . . . ?*
. . . a railway timetable	. . . un horario de trenes *oon orareeo deh tren-es*
. . . information about discounts	. . . información de descuentos *eenformath-yon deh deskwentos*

You may see:

Estación	Station
Largo recorrido	Long distance
Inter-urbano	Inter-City
Cercanías	Local trains
Llegadas	Arrivals
Salidas	Departures
Procedencia ...	Train from ...
Destino	Destination
Andén/vía	Platform
Consigna	Left luggage
Despacho de billetes/ taquilla	Ticket office
Venta inmediata	Tickets on sale for immediate use
Venta anticipada	Advance ticket sales
Entrada	Entrance
Salida	Exit
Facturación de equipajes	Luggage check-in
Horarios	Timetable
Sala de espera	Waiting room

What trains are there for (Madrid) ... ?	¿Qué trenes hay a (Madrid) ... ? *keh tren-es I a (madreed) ... ?*
.. today	... hoy *oy*
.. tomorrow	... mañana *man-yana*
.. on Sunday	... el domingo *el domeengo*

For times, see page 132.

Is it a 'Blue Day'?	¿Es Día Azul? *es deea athool?*
What time does . . . leave?	¿A qué hora sale . . . ? *a keh ora saleh . . . ?*
. . . the next train	. . . el próximo tren *el proxeemo tren*
. . . the first train	. . . el primer tren *el preemair tren*
. . . the last train	. . . el último tren *el ooltimmo tren*
Does it stop in all the stations?	¿Para en todas las estaciones? *para en todas las estath-yones?*
Do I have to change trains/ make a connection?	¿Hay que cambiar de tren/ hacer transbordo? *I keh kamb-yar deh tren/ athair transbordo?*
How long does it take?	¿Cuánto tiempo tarda? *kwanto tee-yempo tarda?*
Is there a supplement?	¿Hay suplemento? *I soopleemento?*

Is/are there . . . ?	¿Hay . . . ? *I . . . ?*
. . . a bar	. . . bar *bar*
. . . couchettes	. . . literas *leeterras*
. . . a children's nursery	. . . coche-guardería *kocheh-gwardareea*
. . . a restaurant car	. . . restaurante *restowranteh*
. . . sleeping compartments	. . . coche-cama *kocheh kama*

At what time does the bar close/open?	¿A qué hora cierra/abre el bar? *a keh ora thee-yerra/abreh el bar?*
Is there a discount for ... ?	¿Hay descuento para ... ? *I deskwento para ... ?*
.. children	... niños *neenyos*
.. students	... estudiantes *estood-yantes*
.. retired people	... jubilados *hoobeelados*

Where is ... ?	¿Dónde está ... ? *dondeh esta ... ?*

.. the left luggage office	... la consigna *la konseegna*
.. the luggage check-in	... facturación de equipajes *faktoorath-yon deh ekeepa-hes*
.. platform (4)	... el andén (4) *el anden (kwatro)*
.. the ticket window	... la taquilla *la takee-ya*
.. the waiting room	... la sala de espera *la sala deh esperra*

Are there any luggage trolleys?	¿Hay carritos para el equipaje? *I kareetos para el ekeepaheh?*

● For directions and asking the way, see page 11.

Which platform does it leave from?	¿De qué andén sale? *deh keh anden saleh?*
Is it delayed?	¿Lleva retraso? *yebba retrasso?*

Buying tickets

Two tickets . . .	Dos billetes . . . *dos beeyet-es . . .*
. . . to Barcelona	. . . para Barcelona *para barthelona*
. . . for the three o'clock Talgo	. . . para el Tago de las tres *para el talgo deh las tres*
Can I reserve a seat?	¿Se puede hacer reserva? *seh pwedeh athair resairba?*
A . . . ticket, please	Un billete . . . , por favor *oon beeyeteh . . . , por fabbor*
single	sencillo *senthee-yo*
return	de ida y vuelta *deh eeda ee bwelta*
first/second class	primera/segunda clase *preemerra/segoonda klasseh*
smoker	fumador *foomador*
non-smoker	no fumador *no foomador*
in couchette	en litera *en leeterra*
in a sleeping compartment	en coche-cama *en kocheh-kama*
and one child's	y uno de niño *ee oono deh neenyo*
How much is that?	¿Cuánto es? *kwanto es?*
Could you write it?	¿Puede escribirlo? *pwedeh eskreebeerlo*
I have a credit/discount card	Tengo tarjeta de crédito/ descuento *tengo tarhetta deh kreditto/ deskwento*

Travel

Luggage

would like . . .	Quiero . . . *kee-yerro* . . .
. . to check this in	. . . facturar esto *faktoorar esto*
. . to leave this	. . . dejar esto *deh-har esto*
Could you help me with my luggage?	¿Puede ayudarme con el equipaje? *pwedeh ayoodarmeh kon el ekeepaheh?*

On the platform

Is this . . . ?	¿Es éste . . . ? *es esteh . . . ?*
. . the train for (Malaga)	. . . el tren para (Málaga) *el tren para (malaga)*
. . the platform for (Barcelona)	. . . el andén para (Barcelona) *el anden para (barthelona)*
. . the second class carriage	. . . el coche de segunda *el kocheh de segoonda*
Where is the . . . carriage?	¿Dónde está el coche . . . ? *dondeh esta el kocheh . . . ?*
. . first class	. . . de primera *deh preemerra*
. . restaurant	. . . restaurante *restowranteh*
I don't have a reservation	No tengo reserva *no tengo resairba*
Excuse me/I'm sorry . . .	Perdone . . . *Pairdoneh* . . .
Is this seat taken?	¿Está ocupado (este asiento)? *esta okoopado (esteh asyento)?*

Could you . . . ?	¿Puede . . . ? *pwedeh . . . ?*
. . . find me a seat	. . . buscarme un asiento *booskarmeh oon as-yento*
. . . tell me when we get to (Malaga)	. . . avisarme cuando lleguemos a (Málaga) *abeesarmeh kwando yegemmos a (malaga)*
Have we arrived?	¿Ya hemos llegado? *ya ehmos yegado?*
This is my seat	Éste es mi asiento *esteh es mee as-yento*
This seat is taken	Este asiento está ocupado *esteh as-yento esta okoopado*

You may hear:

Tiene que cambiar *tee-yenneh keh kamb-yar*	You have to change
Compruebe los datos *komprwebbeh los dattos*	Check the details (on your ticket)
Hay supplemento *I sooplehmento*	There is a supplementary charge
Lleva (media hora) de retraso *yebba (med-ya ora) deh retrasso*	It's (half an hour) late

Is the (Madrid) train running late?	¿Tiene retraso el tren (para Madrid)? *tee-yeneh retrasso el tren (para Madreed)?*
When will it arrive?	¿Cuándo llegará? *kwando yegara?*

By coach

- Most of the signs and information boards found in bus and coach stations are the same as for railway stations (see **By Train** section on page 77).
- Coach travel is cheaper than train travel and the main routes provide a comfortable, fast service. It is advisable to book in advance.
- All towns and villages are linked by a bus or coach service.

Where is the bus station?	¿Dónde está la estación de autobuses? *dondeh esta la estath-yon deh owtobooses?*
When are there buses to (Madrid)?	¿Cuándo hay autobuses a (Madrid)? *kwando I owtobooses a (madreed)?*
A ticket for (Madrid)	Un billete para (Madrid) *oon beeyeteh para (madreed)*
What time does it leave/arrive?	¿A que hora sale/llega? *a keh ora saleh/yegga?*
Are you going by motorway?	¿Va por autopista? *ba por owtopeesta?*
Does it have . . . ?	¿Tiene . . . ? *tee-yenneh . . . ?*
. . air conditioning	. . . aire acondicionado *I-reh akondeeth-yonado*
. . a toilet	. . . servicio *sairbeeth-yo*
Are there any spare places?	¿Hay plazas libres? *I plathas leebres?*
Where does it stop?	¿Dónde para? *dondeh para?*

- For other expressions, see **By Train**, page 77.

By bus and underground

- Spanish towns have a frequent, reliable and relatively cheap bus service (*autobús*). Buses are operated on a flat-fare, 'Pay-as-you-enter' basis and passengers either pay the driver, or insert a single ticket or a multi-journey ticket into an automatic machine.
- Single tickets can be purchased from the driver or from a vendor found at the main bus stops or termini. Most passengers buy a multifare-ticket (*bono-bús*) which can be purchased from ticket vendors, banks, Savings Banks (*Caja de Ahorros*) and some big department stores. They may not be purchased from bus drivers.
- Bus routes are indicated by number (eg *línea* 40) and the route is displayed at each bus stop (*parada*). Buses display the route number and names of the departure and terminus points.
- In the Canary Islands a bus is known as *guagua* (pronounced *wa-wa*). Multi-tickets are known as *bono guagua*.
- Underground systems exist in Madrid and Barcelona. Look for the *METRO* sign. The various lines are indicated by colours and numbers (eg *línea* 2) and direction is indicated by the last station on the line (*dirección*).
- Underground stations open at 6 am and close at 1.30 am.
- Tickets must be inserted into machines at the beginning of the journey. Keep your ticket with you throughout your journey.
- In Madrid, a special travel card (*tarjeta de abono*) can be purchased. This is valid for all three transport systems Bus, Metro and Rail) and is available from tobacconists (*estanco*), and tube and train station ticket points. A monthly ticket (*cupón*) should be purchased with this card and the two are used in conjunction for any journey within the capital within a zone system.

Could you give me . . . ?	Deme . . . *demeh . . .*
. . a book of tickets	. . . un bono-bús *oon bonoboos*
. . a (bus) pass	. . . un abono *oon abono*
. . a travel card	. . . una tarjeta (multiviaje) *oona tarhetta* *(moolteebee-yaheh)*
. . a monthly ticket	. . . un cupón mensual *oon koopon menswal*

Is this the stop for the number 4 bus?	¿Es ésta la parada del autobús número 4? *es esta la parada del owtoboos noomero kwatro?*
Does this bus go (to the centre)?	¿Va este autobús (al centro)? *ba esteh owtoboos (al thentro)?*

● For numbers see page 129.

Do you have a plan (map) . . . ?	¿Tiene un plano . . . ? *tee-yenneh oon plano . . . ?*
. . of the underground	. . . del metro *del metro*
. . of bus routes	. . . de autobuses *deh owtobooses*
Which line should I take to go to (Atocha station)?	¿Qué línea debo tomar para ir a (la estación Atocha)? *keh leen-ya debbo tomar para eer a (la estath-yon atocha)?*
Do I have to change?	¿Tengo que cambiar? *tengo keh kamb-yar?*
Where?	¿Dónde? *dondeh?*
Do you have a timetable?	¿Tiene horario? *tee-yenneh orareeo?*

87

By car

- For car hire see page 15.
- Spanish law requires you to carry your driving licenc
  at all times. If you do not have a pink European
  Communities licence, you will need an International
  Driving licence, which is available from the AA or
  RAC for a small fee.
- Your British insurance will give you only third party
  cover in Spain, whatever cover is valid in the UK. To
  extend this cover, you must have a Green Card,
  details of which are available from your insurance
  company. You should carry this at all times, and it is
  also advisable to carry your vehicle registration
  document.
- A Bail Bond is strongly recommended for driving in
  Spain. Details are available from insurance
  companies or from motoring organisations such as
  the AA or RAC.
- If you drive any vehicle over 75cc capacity you must
  be at least 18 years of age. For motorcycles of less
  than 75cc no permit is necessary and the minimum
  age is 16.
- A GB sticker should be clearly displayed on your
  vehicle.
- Seat belts must be worn on the open road but are not
  obligatory within town limits.
- Crash helmets must be worn by all motorcyclists, an
  dipped headlights used at all times.
- It is against the law to carry a spare can of petrol.
- It is compulsory to carry a spare set of light bulbs for
  each light of the car.
- All Spanish motorways operate on a toll system
  (*peaje*). Prices vary from motorway to motorway.
  Look for the signs *manual* or *automático* depending
  on whether you have the right change. Credit cards
  are not accepted.
- Motorways are indicated by 'A' (for *autopista*)
  followed by the number.
- Main roads are indicated by 'N' (*nacional*) followed
  by the number (sometimes given in Roman

numerals), and secondary roads are indicated by the letter 'C' (*comarcal*) followed by the number.

- The maximum speed limit is 120 kph on motorways (*autopista*), 100 kph on main roads (*carretera nacional*) and 90 kph on other roads. Limits vary between 40 kph and 60 kph in towns. The minimum permitted speed on motorways is 60 kph (kph = kilometres per hour).
- You may be asked to take a breathalyser test in some circumstances.
- Hitch-hiking is legal but difficult. An international hitch-hiker card is available from Edificio España, Grupo 4, Plantall, Madrid 13.
- The *Guardia Civil de Tráfico* patrol the open road. These are different police from the *Guardia Municipal*, who are in charge of traffic in towns.
- In case of an accident there are a number of Red Cross posts (*puestos de Cruz Roja*) attended round the clock.
- Where possible, avoid holiday weekends. Phone the *Dirección General de Tráfico* for information on traffic routes and congestion.

At the petrol station

- Petrol is sold in two grades: *super* (97 octane, the equivalent of 4-star) and *normal* (92 octane, the equivalent of 2-star). Unleaded petrol is not yet widely available in Spain, but this is changing.
- Diesel fuel (*gasoil*) is also available.
- Spanish petrol prices are fixed and uniform.
- Most petrol stations are attended, although self-serve stations are on the increase. Some petrol stations do not give change, especially at night, for security reasons.
- There should be a complaints book (*libro de reclamaciones*) available at all petrol stations.
- Credit cards are not accepted in payment for petrol, but you may be able to obtain 'petrol cheques' at some banks.

Where is there . . . ?	¿Dónde hay . . . ? *dondeh I . . . ?*
. . . a car park	. . . un parking *oon parkeeng*
. . . a garage	. . . un garage *oon garaheh*
. . . a petrol station (gas station)	. . . una gasolinera/estación de servicio *oona gasoleenerra/ estathyon deh serbeethyo*
Fill her up!	Lleno, por favor *yenno, por fabbor*
(Ten) litres of . . .	(Diez) litros de . . . *(dee-yeth) leetros deh . . .*
Two thousand pesetas of . . .	Dos mil pesetas de . . . *dos meel pesetas deh . . .*
. . . 4 star	. . . super *soopair*
. . . 2/3 star	. . . normal *normal*
. . . diesel	. . . gasoil *gasoil*
Do you have lead-free petrol?	¿Tiene gasolina sin plomo? *tee-yenneh gasoleena seen plomo?*
A litre of oil, please	Deme un litro de aceite *dehme oon leetro deh atheyteh*
How much is it?	¿Cuánto es? *kwanto es?*
Do you take . . . ?	¿Aceptan . . . ? *atheptan . . . ?*
. . . petrol cheques	. . . cheques-gasolina *chekes gasoleena*
. . . this voucher	. . . este vale *esteh baleh*

Could you check . . . ?	¿Puede mirar . . . ?
	pwedeh meerar . . . ?
. . the battery	. . . la batería
	la batereea
. . the oil	. . . el aceite
	el atheyteh
. . the radiator	. . . el radiador
	el rad-yador
. . the tyres	. . . los neumáticos
	los noomateekos
. . the windscreen wipers	. . . los limpiaparabrisas
	los leemp-ya-parabreesas
Could you . . . ?	¿Puede . . . ?
	pwedeh . . . ?
. . clean the windows	. . . limpiar los cristales
	leemp-yar los kreestales
. . wash the car	. . . lavar el coche
	labar el kocheh

Problems

I don't have a spare wheel	No tengo rueda de repuesto
	no tengo rooedda deh repwesto
I don't have spare light bulbs	No tengo luces de repuesto
	no tengo loothes deh repwesto
I've run out of petrol	Me he quedado sin gasolina
	meh eh kedado seen gasoleena
Have you got a petrol can?	¿Tiene una lata?
	tee-yenneh oona lata?
My car won't start	Mi coche no arranca
	mee kocheh no aranka

I've had . . .	He tenido . . . *eh teneedo . . .*
. . . an accident	. . . un accidente *oon aktheedenteh*
. . . a breakdown	. . . una avería *oona abereea*
. . . a puncture	. . . un pinchazo *oon peenchatho*
There's a funny noise	Hay un ruido extraño *I oon rooeedo extranyo*
Could you change the wheel/ the bulb?	¿Puede cambiar la rueda/la bombilla? *pwedeh kamb-yar la rooeda/ la bombee-ya?*
The engine has overheated	Se ha calentado el motor *seh a kalentado el motor*
How long will it take?	¿Cuánto tardará? *kwanto tardara?*
It's urgent	Es urgente *es oorhenteh*
I'm . . .	Estoy . . . *estoy . . .*
. . . (10) kilometres away	. . . a (10) kilómetros *a (dee-yeth) keelometros*
. . . on the (Madrid) road	. . . en la carretera de (Madrid) *en la kareterra deh (madreed)*
. . . at kilometre 20	. . . en el kilómetro 20 *en el keelometro beynteh*
It's a (Renault) car	Es un coche marca (Renault) *es oon kocheh marka (renaw*
The registration number is . . .	la matrícula es . . . *la matreekoola es . . .*

- For numbers, see page 129

Can you . . . ?	¿Puede . . . ? *pwedeh . . . ?*
. . . help me	. . . ayudarme *ayoodarmeh*
. . . take me to (a petrol station)	. . . llevarme a (una gasolinera) *yebbarmeh a (oona gasoleenera)*
. . . send a mechanic	. . . mandar a un mecánico *mandar a oon mekaneeko*
. . . send a breakdown lorry	. . . mandar una grúa *mandar oona grooa*
. . . call an ambulance	. . . llamar una ambulancia *yammar oona amboolanth-ya*

At the garage

● Look for the signs *garaje* and *taller*

Do you do repairs?	¿Hacen reparaciones? *athen reparath-yones?*
I don't know what is wrong with it	No sé qué le pasa *no seh keh leh pasa*
I'd like a service	Quiero una puesta a punto *kee-yerro oona pwesta a poonto*
The . . . is broken/doesn't work	. . . está roto/no funciona *esta roto/no foonth-yona*
. . . windscreen	El parabrisas . . . *el parabreesas . . .*
. . . seatbelt	El cinturón . . . *el theentooron . . .*
. . . horn	El claxon . . . *el klaxon . . .*
. . . heater	El calentador . . . *el kalentador . . .*

93

Can you check . . . ?	¿Puede mirar . . . ? *pwedeh meerar . . . ?*
. . . the accelerator	. . . el acelerador *el athelerador*
. . . the brakes	. . . los frenos *los frennos*
. . . the carburettor	. . . el carburador *el karboorador*
. . . the clutch	. . . el embrague *el embrageh*
. . . the engine	. . . el motor *el motor*
. . . the exhaust pipe	. . . el tubo de escape *el toobo deh eskapeh*
. . . the fan belt	. . . la correa del ventilador *la korrea del benteelador*
. . . the gear box	. . . la caja de cambios *la kaha deh kamb-yos*
. . . the handbrake	. . . el freno de mano *el frenno deh mano*
. . . the indicators	. . . los intermitentes *los eentairmeetentes*
. . . the petrol pump	. . . la bomba de gasolina *la bomba deh gasoleena*
. . . the spark plugs	. . . las bujías *las booheeas*
. . . the starter (motor)	. . . el encendido *el enthendeedo*
. . . the steering	. . . la dirección *la deerekth-yon*
. . . the suspension	. . . la suspensión *la soospens-yon*
When will (the car) be ready?	¿Cuándo estará listo (el coche)? *kwando estara leesto (el koche)?*

This is the key . . .	Ésta es la llave . . . *esta es la yabbeh . . .*
. . . to the boot (trunk)	. . . de la maleta *deh la maletta*
. . . to the petrol tank	. . . del depósito de gasolina *del deposeeto deh gasoleena*
Could you give me an estimate/the bill?	¿Puede darme un presupuesto/la factura? *pwedeh darmeh oon presoopwesto/la faktoora?*
Is VAT included?	¿Está incluído el IVA? *esta inklooeedo el eeba?*
Here are the documents	Aquí tiene mis documentos *akee tee-yenneh mees dokoomentos*
Can I have your documents, please?	¿Sus documentos, por favor? *soos dokoomentos, por fabbor?*

You may hear:

¿Dónde está? *dondeh esta?*	Where are you?
¿Qué le pasa? *keh leh pasa?*	What's the matter?
¿Qué marca de coche es? *keh marka deh kocheh es?*	What make of car is it?
Tiene que dejarlo . . . *tee-yenneh keh deh-harlo . . .*	You must leave it . . .
. . . dos días *dos deeas*	. . . for two days
. . . hasta mañana *asta man-yana*	. . . until tomorrow

Travel

You may see:

badén permanente	in constant use (no parking)
calle cortada por obras	road closed for roadworks
carretera particular	private road
ceda el paso	give way
desvío	diversion
estacionamiento (limitado)	(restricted) parking
obras	roadworks
paso a nivel	level crossing
peatones	pedestrians
peaje	toll
prohibido aparcar	no parking
uso obligatorio cinturón de seguridad	seat belt compulsory
zona azul	no parking
zona peatonal	pedestrians only
encienda las luces	switch on lights
apague las luces	switch off lights
vehículos lentos	slow vehicles

Hitch Hiking

Could you give me a lift to . . . ?	¿Puede llevarme a . . . ? *pwedeh yebbarmeh a . . . ?*
Where are you going?	¿A dónde va usted? *a dondeh ba oosted?*
I'll give you something towards the petrol	Le doy algo por la gasolina *le doy algo por la gasoleena*
Could you drop me off here, please?	¿Puede dejarme aquí, por favor? *pwedeh de-harme akee, por fabbor?*

SHOPPING

Opening hours for most shops are from 9.30 or 10 am to 1 pm and again from 4 or 5 pm to 7.30 or 8.30 pm. Large department stores often adopt the same hours but do not close for lunch. Look for the sign *abierto* (open) or *cerrado* (closed).

The larger stores accept credit cards (check first) but in smaller shops it is not common practice to pay by cheque or credit card.

Tourists are entitled to tax refunds on some purchases. Ask for information.

Gift wrapping of goods is customary in most Spanish shops where requested.

In towns and cities it is the practice for some smaller shops (as well as bars and restaurants) to close for the month of July or August. You will see the sign *cerrado por vacaciones* (closed for holidays). Alternatively, some shops close for the afternoon during the summer.

The label PVP (*Precio de Venta al Público*) indicates

retail price and *IVA incluido* indicates that the
Spanish equivalent of VAT is included.
- Open air markets (*rastro* or *mercadillo*) are held once
  or twice a week in most Spanish towns and resorts.
- For currency see **Bank** section, page 113.
- Sales (*Rebajas*, *Liquidación*) take place in January/
  February and July/August.
- Some shops offer free delivery service (including
  food). This service will be indicated by the sign
  Servicio a Domicilio. You can also order from
  supermarkets and grocers by telephone.

Hypermarkets and supermarkets

- Hypermarkets are usually found outside big towns
  and cities and sell everything from food and clothes
  to domestic appliances and car accessories. They are
  rapidly becoming more and more popular and are
  usually cheaper than supermarkets.
- In some supermarkets and hypermarkets you are
  asked to leave your shopping bags at the entrance for
  security reasons. Look for the sign *Deje su Bolso
  Aquí* (Leave your bag here).
- On the way out be prepared for the security officer to
  ask to see inside any handbags you may have with
  you.

I'm just looking, thanks	Estoy mirando, gracias *estoy meerando, grath-yas*
I'm next	Me toca a mí *meh toka a mee*
I'd like this	Quiero eso *kee-yerro eso*
Do you have . . . ?	¿Tiene . . . ? *tee-yenneh . . . ?*
more	más *mas*
less	menos *mennos*

Shopping

You may hear:

¿A quién le toca?
a kee-yen leh toka?

Who's next?

El/la siguiente, por favor
*el/la seeg-yenteh, por
fabbor*

Next, please

¿Qué desea?
keh deseya?

What would you like?

¿En qué puedo servirle?
en keh pwedo sairbeerleh?

How can I help you?

¿Le atienden?
leh at-yenden?

Are you being attended to?

No tenemos/no hay
no tenemmos/no I

We don't have any

No me queda
no meh kedda

I have none left

¿Cuánto quiere?
kwanto kee-yerreh?

How much would you like?

¿Algo más?
algo mas?

Anything else?

¿Se lo envuelvo?
seh lo enbwelbo?

Shall I wrap it?

¿Quiere una bolsa?
kee-yerreh oona bolsa?

Would you like a bag?

Son (500) pesetas
son (keen-yentas) pesetas

That will be (500) pesetas

¿Paga en efectivo o con
tarjeta?
*paga en efekteebo o kon
tarhetta?*

Are you paying by cash or
by credit card?

Pague en caja
pageh en kaha

Please pay at the till

¿A dónde se lo enviamos?
*a dondeh seh lo enbee-
yamos?*

Where shall we send it?

It's very expensive	Es muy caro *es mwee karo*
I'd like something . . .	Quiero algo . . . *kee-yerro algo . . .*
. . . bigger	. . . más grande *mas grandeh*
. . . smaller	. . . más pequeño *mas peken-yo*
. . . cheaper	. . . más barato *mas barato*
Nothing else	Nada más *nada mas*
How much is it?	¿Cuánto es? *kwanto es?*
Could you write it down?	¿Puede escribirlo? *pwedeh eskreebeerlo?*
Do you accept credit cards?	¿Aceptan tarjetas de crédito? *atheptan tarhettas deh kredeeto?*
Could you (gift) wrap it?	¿Puede envolverlo (para regalo)? *pwedeh enbolbairlo (para regalo)?*
Do you have a bag?	¿Tiene una bolsa? *tee-yenneh oona bolsa?*
Could you send it to . . . ?	¿Puede enviarlo a . . . ? *pwedeh enbee-yarlo a . . . ?*

You may see:	
Autoservicio	Self service
Entrada	Entrance
Salida	Way out/exit
Oferta	Special Offer
Caja especial (máximo cinco artículos)	Special till/check out (maximum of 5 items)
Caja	Check-out/till

Shopping for food

- It is very common to do all your shopping in a covered market where you will find a range of stalls to meet your needs.
- Weights and measures: most food is bought by the kilo or fractions of a kilo or otherwise by grammes. A kilo is the equivalent of 2.2 lbs. There are a thousand grammes in a kilo.
  Liquids are bought by the litre. There are about two pints in a litre.
- See Wordlist for individual items.

Can I have . . .	Deme . . . *demeh* . . .
I'd like . . .	Quiero . . . *kee-yerro* . . .
a kilo of . . .	un kilo de . . . *oon keelo deh* . . .
half a kilo of . . .	medio kilo de . . . *med-yo keelo deh* . . .
a packet of . . .	un paquete de . . . *oon paketteh deh* . . .
a jar of . . .	un bote/un tarro de . . . *oon boteh/oon tarro deh* . . .
a bottle of . . .	una botella de . . . *oona boteya deh* . . .
a box of . . .	una caja de . . . *oona kaha deh* . . .
a tin of . . .	una lata de . . . *oona lata deh* . . .
a dozen . . .	una docena de . . . *oona dothenna deh* . . .
half a dozen . . .	media docena de . . . *med-ya dothenna deh* . . .
a slice of . . .	una loncha de . . . *oona loncha deh* . . .

Fruit and Vegetables

● Look for the signs *Frutería/Verdulería* (greengrocers)

Brussels sprouts	coles *koles*
leeks	puerros *pwerros*
(green/red) pepper	pimiento (verde/rojo) *pim-yento (bairdeh/roho)*
a head of garlic	una cabeza de ajos *oona kabetha deh ahos*
grapes (green/black)	uvas (blancas/negras) *oobas (blankas/neggras)*

At the grocers

● Look for the signs *Comestibles, Ultramarinos* or *Alimentación.* These are shops which sell everything from tinned food to wine and bread.

decaffeinated/instant coffee	café descafeinado/ instantáneo *kafeh deskafeynado/* *eenstantanyo*
(olive) oil	aceite (de oliva) *atheyteh (deh oleeba)*
(drinking) yogurt	yogur (para beber) *yogoor (para bebair)*
stock cubes	cubitos de caldo *koobeetos deh kaldo*
(powdered) milk	leche (en polvo) *lecheh (en polvo)*
tomato puree	tomate frito *tomateh freeto*
some tea bags	unas bolsitas de té *oonas bolseetas deh teh*
a bar of chocolate	una tableta de chocolate *oona tabletta deh chokolateh*

Snacks and aperitifs

- Many of these snacks can be obtained in bars. They are known generally as *tapas* and are sometimes included in the price of the drinks.

tuna fish (in oil)	atún (en aceite) *atoon (en atheyteh)*
green/black/stuffed olives	olivas verdes/negras/rellenas *oleebas bairdes/negras/ reyennas*
olives without the stone	olivas sin hueso *oleebas seen wesso*
cheese sticks	palitos de queso *paleetos deh kesso*
hazelnuts	avellanas *abeyanas*
peanuts	cacahuetes *kakawettes*
sunflower seeds	pipas *peepas*

At the butcher's and delicatessen

- Look for *Charcutería*, *Salchichería* (butcher's delicatessen). Also *embutidos* (cold meats, especially pork).
- You can buy this sort of thing in a grocer's store or in a *Mantequería* (delicatessen).

bacon	bacón/tocino *bakon/totheeno*
ham	jamón de York *hamon deh york*
pâté	paté *pateh*
cheese in portions	quesitos *keseetos*

103

. . . cheese	queso . . . *kesso . . .*
soft . . .	. . . blando/tierno *blando/tee-yairno*
hard . . .	. . . duro *dooro*
mild . . .	. . . suave *swabeh*
strong . . .	. . . fuerte *fwairteh*
goat's . . .	. . . de cabra *deh kabra*
round shaped, mild . . .	. . . de bola *deh bola*
hard (from ewe's milk) . . .	. . . manchego *mancheggo*

Spanish specialities

jamón serrano *hamon seranno*	cured/smoked ham
longaniza *longaneetha*	spicy sausage with herbs
butifarra *booteefara*	large sausage
morcilla *morthee-ya*	black pudding
mortadela *mortadella*	cold meat
requesón *rekehson*	cottage/curd cheese

At the baker's

- Look for the signs *Panadería* (baker's), *pan* (bread) and *horno* (oven).
- Most baker's also sell milk and soft drinks, ice cream, cakes and sweets.

a long loaf	una barra *oona barra*
a . . . loaf	un pan . . . *oon pan . . .*
. . . large	. . . grande *grandeh*
. . . medium	. . . mediano/a *med-yano/a*
. . . small	. . . pequeño/a *peken-yo/a*
sliced bread	pan inglés/de molde *pan in-gles/deh moldeh*
a bread roll	un panecillo *oon panethee-yo*
a bun	un bollo *oon boyo*

Milk

- Look for *Lechería*. Milk is also sold in baker's, grocer's or supermarkets but is not delivered to your door.

A bottle of . . . milk, please	Una botella de leche . . . por favor *oona botteya deh lecheh . . . por fabbor*
. . . full cream	. . . entera *enterra*
. . . semi-skimmed	. . . semidesnatada *semeedesnatada*
. . . skimmed	. . . desnatada *desnatada*

Cakes and sweets

- Look for *Pastelería* (cake shop), *Confitería*, *Bombonería* or *Dulces*. They all sell sweets.
- A *Churrería* is a shop selling *churros*, *buñuelos* and crisps to take away.
- You can buy *churros* by the peseta. A *churro* is a long strip of fried pastry sprinkled with sugar. They are best eaten when they are hot and are very popular dipped in hot chocolate.
- *Buñuelos* are another kind of fritter, round in shape.
- Cakes can be bought singly but it is more common to buy them by the half dozen (*media docena*), the dozen (*docena*) or by weight. Types of cake often vary from region to region and there are also seasonal differences as well as cakes made for special festivals.
- If you don't know the name, point and say *Quiero eso, por favor*. If you want a cake typical of the region say *Quiero un pastel típico de aquí*.

200 pesetas of churros, please	Doscientas pesetas de churros, por favor *dosthee-yentas pesetas deh chooros, por fabbor*
small candied egg yolks	yemas *yemmas*
chocolates	bombones *bombones*
mints	caramelos de menta *karamellos deh menta*

Ice cream

- Look for *Heladería* (Ice-cream parlour) or *helados* (ice-cream).

a cornet	un barquillo *oon barkeeyo*
a (chocolate) iced lolly	un polo (de bombón) *oon polo (deh bombon)*
a wafer	un corte *oon korteh*

Shopping

Meat

Look for *Carnicería* (butcher's).

loin	lomo *lomo*
steak	filete *feeletteh*
meat for stew	carne para estofado *karneh para estofado*
a joint for roasting	una pieza para asar *oona pee-yetha para asar*
I want it boneless/without fat	Lo quiero sin hueso/sin grasa *lo kee-yerro seen wesso/seen grasa*
minced meat	carne picada *karneh peekada*

Chicken and poultry

Look for *Pollería* and *Pollo*.

whole	entero *enterro*
in pieces	a trozos *a trothos*
chicken breasts	pechugas de pollo *pechoogas deh poyo*
chicken legs	muslos de pollo *mooslos deh poyo*

Fish and seafood

Look for *Pescadería* (fishmonger's), *Pescados* (fish) and *Mariscos* (seafood).

Spain is very rich in fish and seafood. You will find many varieties that you may not have seen before and will want to try. Just point and say '*Ese pescado, por favor*'.

eels	anguilas *angeelas*
hake	merluza *mairlootha*
red mullet	salmonetes *salmonettes*
sprats	sardineta *sardeenetta*
whitebait	boquerones *bokehron-es*
(big) prawns	langostinos *langosteenos*
shrimps	quisquillas *keeskee-yas*
Please, can you . . . ?	Por favor, ¿puede . . . ? *por fabbor, pwedeh . . . ?*
. . . clean it	. . . limpiarlo *limp-yarlo*
. . . fillet it	. . . cortarlo a filetes *kortarlo a feelet-es*
. . . take the bones out	. . . quitar la raspa *keetar la raspa*

At the tobacconist's

● Look for *Estanco* or *Tabacos*, where you can buy
  tobacco, stamps, postcards and sweets. You can buy
  dark or light tobacco. The Spanish brand names are
  much cheaper than the imported brands.

A packet of cigarettes	Un paquete de cigarrillos . . . *oon paketeh deh* *theegareeyos . . .*
a box of matches	una caja de cerillas *oona kaha deh thereeyas*
a packet of cigars	un paquete de puros *oon paketeh deh pooros*

At the chemist's

- Look for *Farmacia* and a red or green cross symbol. There is a rota system of chemists which remain open for 24 hours (*Farmacia de Guardia*).
- Chemists sell medical supplies and a limited selection of toiletries. You will find a wider range of the latter in a *Perfumería* or *Droguería* (drugstore).
- See also page 68, **At the Doctor's**.

have this prescription	Tengo esta receta *tengo esta rethetta*
baby food	comida para niños *komeeda para neenyos*
insect repellent	loción para insectos *loth-yon para insektos*
plasters	tiritas *teereetas*
throat pastilles	pastillas para la garganta *pasteeyas para la garganta*
I'd like something for ...	Quiero algo para ... *kee-yerro algo para ...*

Buying toiletries

- Look for *Droguería* (drugstore) or *Perfumería*, sometimes called *Droguería-Perfumería*. These sell toiletries and also household goods.

handcream	crema para las manos *kremma para las manos*
lipsalve	cacao para los labios *kakow para los lab-yos*
make-up remover	crema limpiadora *kremma leemp-yadora*
paper tissues	pañuelos de papel *panwellos deh papel*

Self catering and camping equipment

- Look for *Droguería* (see above), *Ferretería* (the nearest British equivalent is the hardware store) and *Deportes* (sports shop). Adaptors and other electrical goods can be bought in *Electro-Domésticos* (electrical goods).

a drying-up cloth	un paño de cocina *oon panyo deh kotheena*
an insecticide	un insecticida *oon eensekteetheeda*
kitchen roll	un rollo de papel de cocina *oon royo deh papel deh kotheena*
some rubbish bags	bolsas de basura *bolsas deh basoora*
a scouring pad	un estropajo *oon estropaho*
tent pegs	estacas de camping *estakas deh kampeeng*

Beach and photographic items

- You can buy beach items at sports shops, and general stores. Look for the sign *Artículos de Playa*.
- Photographic films cannot always be bought in chemists. Look for photographic specialists and in the *Fotografía* section of department stores.
- Buying and developing film is a lot more expensive in Spain.

a black and white film	un rollo en blanco y negro *oon royo en blanko ee negro*
a colour film	un rollo en color *oon royo en kolor*

for prints	para fotos
	para fotos
for slides	para diapositivas
	para deeaposeeteebas

Please can you . . . ?	Por favor, ¿puede . . . ?
	por fabbor pwedeh . . . ?
. . . develop the film	. . . revelar el rollo
	rebelar el royo
. . . load the camera	. . . poner el rollo
	ponair el royo
. . . take the film out	. . . sacar el rollo
	sakkar el royo
. . . repair the camera	. . . reparar la cámara
	reparar la kamera

The film is stuck	El rollo esta atascado
	el royo esta ataskado
When will they be ready?	¿Cuándo estarán hechas?
	kwando estaran echas?

At the stationer's

If you wish to buy stationery, magazines, newspapers etc look for *Librería* (bookshop/stationers), *Papelería* (stationers), *Kiosco* (kiosk), or *Estanco* (tobacconist).

Where are the English books?	¿Dónde están los libros ingleses?
	dondeh estan los leebros ingleses?

Presents

Look for *Regalos* (gifts), *Bazar* (bazaar), *Joyería* (jeweller's), *Tienda de Regalos* (gift shop), *Souvenirs*.

Clothes

- Look for *Boutique*, *Confecciones Señora* (women's clothes shop), *Confecciones Caballero* (men's clothes shop), *Modas* (fashion clothes). For leather goods look for *Artículos de Piel* or *Cuero*.
- For sizes, colours, materials, patterns etc see **Essential Information**.

I'd like size 40	Quiero la talla 40 *kee-yerro la ta-ya kwarenta*
Can I try it (them) on?	¿Puedo probármelo(s)? *pwedo probarmelo(s)?*
Where is the fitting room?	¿Dónde está el probador? *dondeh esta el probador?*
It doesn't (they don't) fit	No me va(n) bien *no meh ba(n) bee-yen*
I'll take it (them)	Me lo(s) quedo *meh lo(s) kedo*

Shoes and shoe repairs

- Look for *Zapatería*, *Calzados* (shoe shop) and *Zapatos* (shoes).
- For repairs look for *Reparación de Calzado*.

Have you got these shoes in black?	¿Tiene esos zapatos en negro? *tee-yenneh esos thapatos en neggro?*
Can you repair these shoes?	¿Puede reparar estos zapatos? *pwedeh reparar estos thapatos?*
Can you put on a new heel/sole?	¿Puede poner un tacón nuevo/una suela nueva? *pwedeh ponair oon takon nwebbo/oona swella nwebba?*
When will they be ready?	¿Cuándo estarán listos? *kwando estaran leestos?*
Do you have shoe polish?	¿Tiene betún? *tee-yenneh betoon?*

At the bank

- Normal banking hours are from 9am to 2pm on weekdays and on Saturdays from 9am to 1pm, although some banks close on Saturdays during the summer. You can change money in normal banks (*Banco*) and also in a savings bank (*Caja de Ahorros*). For reasons of security many banks employ the use of an entry bell which customers press before they are let in.
- When changing traveller's cheques or Eurocheques you will need to have your passport with you, though not if you want to change cash. Look for the sign *Cambio* or *Extranjero*. Banks display the exchange rates of most currencies. Look for the sign *Libra Esterlina* for pounds sterling and *Dólares* for dollars.
- The clerk will work out the exchange and commission (this varies from bank to bank) and will then send you to a till (*Caja*) to collect your money.

113

- In some of the bigger cities there are branches of the major British banks. Check services available with your own bank before you travel.
- Currency: Spanish coins (*monedas*) are in units of 1, 2, 5, 10, 25, 50, 100, 200, and 500 pesetas, whilst bank notes (*billetes*) are issued in 200, 500, 1000, 2000, 5000 and 10,000 peseta denominations.
- A coin of five pesetas is known as a *duro*. You may hear Spaniards sometimes refer to currency in terms of *duros*. 25 pesetas then become five *duros*.

I'd like to change . . .	Quiero cambiar . . . *kee-yerro kamb-yar . . .*
. . . these pounds (sterling)	. . . estas libras *estas leebras*
. . . these dollars	. . . estos dólares *estos dolares*
. . . these francs	. . . estos francos *estos frankos*
. . . this into pesetas	. . . esto en pesetas *esto en pesetas*
. . . this into pounds	. . . esto en libras *esto en leebras*
. . . this into escudos	. . . esto en escudos *esto en eskoodos*
I'd like to cash . . .	Quiero cobrar . . . *kee-yerro kobrar . . .*
. . . these traveller's cheques	. . . estos cheques de viaje *estos chek-es deh bee-aheh*
. . . these eurocheques	. . . estos eurocheques *estos eurochek-es*
. . . this cheque	. . . este cheque *esteh chekeh*
What is the exchange rate?	¿A cómo está el cambio? *a komo esta el kamb-yo?*

It's . . .   Son . . .
                               son . . .

. . . three hundred pounds   . . . trescientas libras
                               tres-thee-yentas leebras

. . . five hundred dollars   . . . quinientos dólares
                               keen-yentos dolares

● For numbers see page 129.

How much commission do   ¿Cuánto cobran de comisión?
you charge?   *kwanto kobran deh komees-*
                               yon?

Do you want . . . ?   ¿Quiere . . . ?
                               kee-yerreh . . . ?

. . . my passport   . . . mi pasaporte
                               mee pasaporteh

. . . my Eurocheque card   . . . mi tarjeta Eurocheque
                               mee tarhetta eurochek-eh

Where do I sign?   ¿Dónde firmo?
                               dondeh feermo?

Can you give me . . .   Deme . . .
                               dehmeh . . .

. . small notes   . . . billetes pequeños
                               beeyet-es pekenyos

. . coins   . . . moneda
                               moneda

. . change   . . . cambio
                               kamb-yo

Can I use this card?   ¿Puedo usar esta tarjeta?
                               pwedo oosar esta tarhetta?

Could you call/telex my   ¿Puede llamar/poner un telex
bank?   a mi banco?
                               pwedeh yamar/ponair oon
                               telex a mee banko?

Has some money arrived for   ¿Ha llegado una transferencia
me?   para mí?
                               a yegado oona transferenth-
                               ya para mee?

I've lost . . .	He perdido . . .
	eh pairdeedo . . .

. . . some traveller's cheques	. . . unos cheques de viaje
	oonos chek-es deh bee-aheh

. . . some Eurocheques	. . . unos Eurocheques
	oonos eurochek-es

. . . my (credit) card	. . . mi tarjeta (de crédito)
	mee tarhetta (deh kreditto)

. . . my cheque book	. . . mi talonario
	mee talonar-yo

I'd like to . . .	Quiero . . .
	kee-yerro . . .

. . . open a savings account	. . . abrir una cuenta de ahorro
	abreer oona kwenta deh a-orro

. . . open a current account	. . . abrir una cuenta corriente
	abreer oona kwenta koree-yenteh

. . . pay this in to my account	. . . ingresar esto a mi cuenta
	ingressar esto a mee kwenta

. . . withdraw (15,000) pesetas from my account	. . . sacar (quince mil) pesetas de mi cuenta
	sakar (keentheh meel) pesetas deh mee kwenta

. . . transfer some money	. . . hacer una transferencia
	athair oona transferenth-ya

. . . send a giro	. . . mandar un giro
	mandar oon heero

...ere is/are ...	Aquí tiene ... *akee tee-yenneh* ...
... my residence permit	... mi permiso de residencia *mee pairmeeso deh reseedenth-ya*
... the details	... los datos *los dattos*
...ould you tell me the balance ... f my account?	¿Puede decirme el saldo de mi cuenta? *pwedeh detheermeh el saldo deh mee kwenta?*

You may hear:

Firme aquí *feermeh akee*	Sign here
Su pasaporte, por favor *soo pasaporteh, por fabbor*	Your passport, please
Pase por caja/a la ventanilla de pagos *paseh por kaha/a la ventaneeya de pagos*	Could you go to the till?
Este papel es para usted *esteh papel es para oosted*	This paper is for you
¿Puede ... ? *pwedeh ... ?*	Could you ... ?
... esperar un momento *esperar oon momento*	... wait a moment
... rellenar esto *reyennar esto*	... fill this out
¿Cómo se llama usted? *komo seh yama oosted?*	What is your name?

117

Business expressions

I'd like to speak to ...	Quisiera hablar con ... *kees-yerra ablar kon ...*

I have an appointment with ...	Tengo una cita con ... *tengo oona theeta kon ...*
... the director	... el director *el dirrektor*
... the manager	... el gerente *el herrenteh*
... the personnel manager	... el jefe de personal *el hefeh deh pairsonal*
... the sales manager	... el jefe de ventas *el hefeh deh bentas*

I need ...	Necesito ... *netheseeto ...*
... a secretary	... un secretario/una secretaria *oon sekretaryo/oona sekretarya*
... an interpreter	... un/una intérprete *oon/oona eentairpreteh*
... a translator	... un traductor/una traductora *oon tradooktor/oona tradooktora*

Can you ... ?	¿Puede ... ? *pwedeh ... ?*
... cancel my appointment with ...	... cancelar mi cita con ... *kanthelar mee theeta kon ...*
... make another appointment	... fijar otra cita *fee-har otra theeta*

118 ● For other business expressions, see page 64.

At the post office

Look for the sign *Correos* and the symbol

There is no need to go to a post office if you only
want to buy stamps. Buy these in a tobacconist's
(*Estanco*).

Post office opening hours are usually similar to shop
opening hours: 9am–1pm and 4pm–7pm during the
week, and on Saturday mornings.

The different sections are found under the following
signs: *Certificados* (recorded delivery), *Venta de
Sellos* (stamps), *Telegramas* (telegrams), *Paquetes*
(parcels), *Giros* (if you wish to cash a National
Girobank Postcheque on your own Post Office
account or send money).

If you wish to receive *post restante* mail, the sender
should address the letter with your name, *Lista de
Correos*, the name of the town or village, and the
name of the province.

a stamp for England/the United States	Un sello para Inglaterra/ Estados Unidos *oon seh-yo para inglaterra/ estados ooneedos*
Two (30 pesetas) stamps	Dos sellos (de treinta pesetas) *dos seh-yos (deh treynta pesetas)*
I'd like to send this . . .	Quiero mandar . . . *kee-yerro mandar . . .*
. . letter	. . . esta carta *esta karta*
. . parcel	. . . este paquete *esteh paketteh*
. . postcard	. . . esta postal *esta postal*

119

by airmail	por avión *por ab-yon*
by surface mail	por correo normal *por koreyo normal*
first class	urgente *oorhenteh*
by recorded delivery	certificado/a *thairteefeekado/a*
Is there a giro/parcel for me?	¿Hay un giro/un paquete par mí? *I oon heero/oon paketteh para mee?*
I'd like a post office box	Quiero un apartado de correos *kee-yerro oon apartado deh koreos*
I'd like to send a giro/a telegram to this address	Quiero mandar un giro/pone un telegrama a esta dirección *kee-yerro mandar oon heero, ponair oon telegrama a esta deerekth-yon*
How much does it cost per word?	¿Cuánto cuesta por palabra? *kwanto kwesta por palabra?*
How long will it take to arrive?	¿Cuánto tardará en llegar? *kwanto tardara en yeggar?*

You may hear:	
Vaya a aquella ventanilla *baya a akehya bentaneeya*	Please go to that window
Rellene este impreso/ formulario *reyenneh esteh eempreso/ formoolar-yo*	Please fill in this form
Ponga la dirección aquí *ponga la deerekth-yon akee*	Please put the address here
No puede enviarlo así *no pwedeh enbee-yarlo asee*	You can't send it like that

Telephoning

- Telephone boxes have clear displays of international phone codes and operating instructions in a number of languages including English.
- For international calls you may use 50 peseta coins or 100 peseta coins, depending on the kind of phone box you are using. For local calls use 5 peseta or 25 peseta coins.
- You may also make phone calls from a central telephone exchange (*la Telefónica*). The attendant will tell you which booth to use. Payment is made after the call.
- To phone the UK, dial 07, wait for a sharp tone, then dial 44 plus the remaining code without the initial 0.
- Some small towns and villages install special seasonal telephones in the summer to cater for touristic demand. These are attended by telephonists who make the connection and charge you accordingly.
- If you phone from a hotel you will be charged extra.

Is there a phone box near here?	¿Hay una cabina por aquí? *I oona kabeena por akee?*
Can I use the phone?	¿Puedo usar el teléfono? *pwedo oosar el telefono?*
Where is the phone?	¿Dónde está el teléfono? *dondeh esta el telefono?*
Do you have the phone book?	¿Tiene la guía telefónica? *tee-yenneh la geea telefonikka?*
What is the code for (London)?	¿Qué prefijo es para (Londres)? *keh prehfee-ho es para (londres)?*
Can I speak to . . . ?	¿Puedo hablar con . . . ? *pwedo ablar kon . . . ?*
Could I have extension . . .	Quiero la extensión . . . *kee-yerro la extens-yon . . .*
I'll call back later	Llamaré más tarde *yamareh mas tardeh*

It's (Mrs Smith) (informal)	Soy (la señora Smith) *soy (la senyora smeeth)*
It's (Miss Smith) (formal)	De parte de (la señorita Smith) *deh parteh deh (la senyoreeta smeeth)*
Can I leave a message?	¿Puedo dejar un recado? *pwedo deh-har oon rekado?*
Can you ask him/her to call me?	¿Puede decirle que me llame? *pwedeh detheerleh keh meh yameh?*
My number is ...	Mi número es ... *mee noomero es ...*
I'm sorry, I've got the wrong number	Perdone, me he equivocado de número *pairdoneh, meh eh ekeevokado deh noomero*

Talking to the operator

Could you ... ?	¿Puede ... ? *pwedeh ... ?*
... give me Mr Smith's number	... darme el número del señor Smith *darmeh el noomero del senyor smeeth*
... tell me the cost of the call	... decirme cuánto es la llamada *detheermeh kwanto es la yamada*
I've been cut off	Se ha cortado la línea *seh a kortado la leenya*
Can I pay by card?	¿Puedo pagar con tarjeta? *pwedo pagar kon tarhetta?*
I'd like to reverse the charges	Quiero llamar a cobro revertido *kee-yerro yamar a kobro rebairteedo*

● For communication problems, see page 60.

Answering the phone

Hello	Dígame *deegameh*
It's me	Soy yo *soy yo*
One moment, please	Un momento, por favor *oon momento, por fabbor*

You may hear:

Hay una llamada para usted *I oona yamada para oosted*	There is a call for you
¿Quiere dejar un recado? *kee-yerreh deh-har oon rekado?*	Would you like to leave a message?
Se ha equivocado de número *seh a ekeebokado deh noomero*	You have the wrong number
¿Cuál es su número? *kwal es soo noomero?*	What's your number?
No cuelgue *no kwelgeh*	Don't hang up
No contesta *no kontesta*	There is no answer
Comunica/está comunicando *komooneeka/esta komooneekando*	It's engaged
Hable *ableh*	Speak now, please
Las líneas están ocupadas *las leenyas estan okoopadas*	The lines are busy
Espere, por favor *esperreh, por fabbor*	Can you hold, please
Lo intentaré otra vez *lo intentareh otra beth*	I'll try again

123

Police

- There are three separate police forces in Spain, each with their own distinctive uniforms and each with different, clearly defined duties.
- The function of *Policía Municipal* is mainly to carry out traffic police duties in towns.
- *Policía Nacional*, now merged with *Cuerpo Superior de Policía*, is the main police force and operates in the larger towns and cities. If you need to find a police station look for the sign *Comisaría*.
- *Guardia Civil* are responsible for law and order and traffic in the countryside and in towns of less than 20,000 inhabitants.
- If you lose your passport, you must report it quickly and ask the police for a certificate (*certificado*) which you can then take to the consulate or embassy. Other reported lost goods or belongings also require a certificate for insurance purposes.
- If you need a residence or work permit you also need to make enquiries at a police station.
- If you are unlucky enough to be arrested you have the right to a lawyer and an interpreter. The police should inform your consulate or embassy of your arrest.
- Ask at the airport or in the tourist office for a brochure produced by the police in different languages on safety and security for tourists.
- Lost property should find its way to the lost property office (*Oficina de Objetos Perdidos*) in the town hall (*Ayuntamiento*).
- If you require a special visa or work permit, obtain these in advance from the Spanish Consulate, 20 Draycott Place, London SW3.

My son/daughter is lost	Mi hijo/hija se ha perdido *mee ee-ho/ee-ha seh a pairdeedo*
My friend has disappeared	Mi amigo/a ha desaparecido *mee ameego/a a desaparetheedo*

ve lost . . .	He perdido . . . *eh pairdeedo . . .*
omeone has stolen . . .	Me han robado . . . *meh an robado . . .*
. . my camera	. . . la cámara *la kamara*
. . my car	. . . el coche *el kocheh*
. my car radio	. . . la radio del coche *la radyo del kocheh*
. my jewels	. . . las joyas *las hoyas*
. my luggage	. . . el equipaje *el ekeepaheh*
. my money	. . . el dinero *el dinerro*
. my purse	. . . el monedero *el monederro*
. my wallet	. . . la cartera *la karterra*
. my airline tickets	. . . los billetes de avión *los beeyetes deh ab-yon*
. my (car) keys	. . . las llaves (del coche) *las yabbes del kocheh*
. my driving licence	. . . el carnet de conducir *el karnay deh kondootheer*
. my watch	. . . el reloj *el reloh*
left it in the hotel/a taxi	Lo he dejado en el hotel/ en un taxi *lo eh de-hado en el otel/en oon taxee*

It happened . . .	Ha sido . . . *a seedo . . .*
. . . a moment ago	. . . hace un momento *atheh oon momento*
. . . this morning	. . . esta mañana *esta man-yana*
. . . in the underground	. . . en el metro *en el metro*
. . . in the street	. . . en la calle *en la ka-yeh*
It was a man/woman	Fue un hombre/una mujer *fweh oon ombreh/oona moohair*
I don't know who it was	No sé quién fue *no seh kee-yen fweh*
I don't know . . . it happened	No se . . . fue *no seh . . . fweh*
. . . when	. . . cuándo *kwando*
. . . where	. . . dónde *dondeh*
. . . how	. . . cómo *komo*

● For other expressions of time, see page 132.

Descriptions

tall	alto/a *alto/a*
short	bajo/a *baho/a*
medium height	mediano/a *med-yano/a*
fat	gordo/a *gordo/a*

thin	delgado/a *delgado/a*
dark	moreno/a *morenno/a*
blonde	rubio/a *roob-yo/a*
red haired	pelirrojo/a *pelee-roho/a*
with … eyes	de ojos … *deh ohos …*
… blue	… azules *athool-es*
… green	… verdes *baird-es*
… brown	… castaños *kastanyos*
… dark	… negros *neggros*
with … hair	de pelo … *deh pelo …*
… short	… corto *korto*
… long	… largo *largo*
… straight	… liso *leeso*
… curly	… rizado *reethado*
bearded	con barba *kon barba*
with a moustache	con bigote *kon beegoteh*

Services

(slightly) bald	(un poco) calvo *(oon poko) kalbo*
He/she was wearing . . .	Llevaba . . . *yebaba . . .*
. . . glasses	. . . gafas *gafas*
. . . a blue jersey	. . . jersey azul *hairseh athool*
I'm lost	Me he perdido *meh eh pairdeedo*
Could you call the British Consulate?	Por favor, llame al Consulado Británico *por fabbor, yameh al konsoolado britanikko*

You may hear:

Deme los datos, por favor *demeh los dattos, por fabbor*	Could you give me all the details
¿Cómo es? *komo es?*	What is he/she/it like?
¿Cuándo . . . ? *kwando . . . ?*	When . . . ?
¿Dónde . . . ? *dondeh . . . ?*	Where . . . ?
¿Cómo . . . ? *komo . . . ?*	How . . . ?
¿Quién . . . ? *kee-yen . . . ?*	Who . . . ?
. . . fue/ha sido *fweh/a seedo*	. . . was it
Aquí no está *akee no esta*	It's not here
Le avisaremos *leh abeesaremmos*	We'll let you know

128 • For giving personal details, see page 62.

Cardinal numbers

0	cero *thero*		15	quince *keentheh*
1	uno *oono*		16	dieciséis *dee-yethee-seys*
2	dos *dos*		17	diecisiete *dee-yethee-see-yeteh*
3	tres *tres*		18	dieciocho *dee-yethee-ocho*
4	cuatro *kwatro*		19	diecinueve *dee-yethee-nwebbeh*
5	cinco *theenko*		20	veinte *beynteh*
6	seis *seys*		21	veintiuno *beyntee-oono*
7	siete *see-yeteh*		30	treinta *treynta*
8	ocho *ocho*		40	cuarenta *kwarenta*
9	nueve *nwebbeh*		50	cincuenta *thinkwenta*
10	diez *dee-yeth*		60	sesenta *sesenta*
11	once *ontheh*		70	setenta *setenta*
12	doce *dotheh*		80	ochenta *ochenta*
13	trece *tretheh*		90	noventa *nobenta*
14	catorce *katortheh*		100	cien *thee-yen*

Ordinal numbers

1st	primero *preemero*	**4th**	cuarto *kwarto*
2nd	segundo *segoondo*	**5th**	quinto *keento*
3rd	tercero *tairthero*	**6th**	sexto *sexto*

Days of the week

Monday	lunes *loon-es*	**Friday**	viernes *bee-yairn-es*
Tuesday	martes *mart-es*	**Saturday**	sábado *sabaddo*
Wednesday	miércoles *mee-yairkol-es*	**Sunday**	domingo *domeengo*
Thursday	jueves *hweb-es*		

Months

January	enero *enerro*	**July**	julio *hoolyo*
February	febrero *febrerro*	**August**	agosto *agosto*
March	marzo *martho*	**September**	septiembre *set-yembreh*
April	abril *abreel*	**October**	octubre *oktoobreh*
May	mayo *my-o*	**November**	noviembre *nob-yembreh*
June	junio *hoonyo*	**December**	diciembre *deeth-yembreh*

Public holidays

anuary 1st	Año Nuevo	New Year's Day
anuary 6th	Día de Reyes (Epifanía)	Epiphany
March 19th	San José	St Joseph's Day
March or April	Jueves Santo Viernes Santo Semana Santa	Maundy Thursday Good Friday Easter
May 1st	Día del Trabajo	Labour Day
May or June	Corpus Christi	Corpus Christi
uly 25th	Día de Santiago	St James's Day
ugust 15th	La Asunción	Assumption Day
October 12th	Día de La Hispanidad (Día del Pilar)	Columbus Day
November 1st	Día de Todos los Santos	All Saint's Day
December 6th	Día de La Constitución	Constitution Day
December 8th	La Inmaculada Concepción	Immaculate Conception
December 25th	Día de Navidad	Christmas Day

Colours

lack	negro/a *neggro/a*	pink	rosa *rosa*	
lue	azul *athool*	red	rojo/a *roho/a*	
rown	marrón *marron*	white	blanco/a *blanko/a*	
reen	verde *bairdeh*	yellow	amarillo/a *amareeyo/a*	
rey	gris *grees*	orange	naranja *naranha*	

131

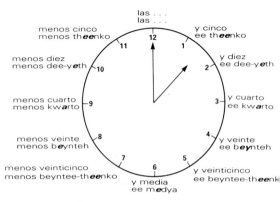

las . . .
las . . .

menos cinco
menos th**ee**nko

y cinco
ee th**ee**nko

menos diez
menos dee-y**e**th

y diez
ee dee-y**e**th

menos cuarto
menos kw**a**rto

y cuarto
ee kw**a**rto

menos veinte
menos b**ey**nteh

y veinte
ee b**ey**nteh

menos veinticinco
menos beyntee-th**ee**nko

y veinticinco
ee beyntee-th**ee**nk

y media
ee m**e**dya

What time is it?	¿Qué hora es? *keh ora es?*
It's one o'clock	Es la una *es la oona*
It's two o'clock	Son las dos *son las dos*
It's a quarter past three	Son las tres y cuarto *son las tres ee kwarto*
It's twenty to eleven	Son las once menos veinte *son las ontheh menos beynte*
. . . am	. . . de la mañana *deh la man-yana*
. . . pm (afternoon/evening)	. . . de la tarde *deh la tardeh*
. . . pm (evening/night)	. . . de la noche *deh la nocheh*
midday	mediodía *med-yodeea*
midnight	medianoche *med-yanocheh*
At what time . . . ?	¿A qué hora . . . ? *a keh ora . . . ?*

At six o'clock	A las seis *a las seys*
In five minutes	En cinco minutos *en theenko minootos*
Half an hour ago	Hace media hora *atheh med-ya ora*
Today	hoy *oy*
Yesterday	ayer *ayair*
Tomorrow	mañana *man-yana*
In the morning	por la mañana *por la man-yana*
In the afternoon/evening	por la tarde *por la tardeh*
At night	por la noche *por la nocheh*
Last night	anoche *anocheh*
This morning	esta mañana *esta man-yana*
This afternoon/evening	esta tarde *esta tardeh*
Tonight	esta noche *esta nocheh*
The day before yesterday	anteayer *anteh-ayair*
The day after tomorrow	pasado mañana *pasado man-yana*
Next week	la semana que viene *la semana keh bee-yenneh*
Next Monday	el lunes próximo *el loon-es proxeemo*
Last Monday	el lunes pasado *el loon-es pasado*

133

on Monday	el lunes *el loon-es*
on Mondays	los lunes *los loon-es*
before	antes *ant-es*
after	después *despwes*
until	hasta *asta*
during	durante *dooranteh*
(at) the beginning . . .	(a) principios . . . *(a) preentheep-yos*
(in) the middle . . .	(a) mediados . . . *(a) med-yados . . .*
(at) the end . . .	(a) finales . . . *(a) feenal-es . . .*
. . . of August	. . . de agosto *deh agosto*
What's the date today?	¿A qué fecha estamos? *a keh fecha estamos?*
It's . . .	Es . . . *es . . .*
. . . the 1st of May	. . . el uno de mayo *el oono deh my-o*
. . . the 5th of April	. . . el cinco de abril *el theenko deh abreel*

Seasons

Spring	primavera *preemaberra*	**Autumn**	otoño *otonyo*
Summer	verano *berano*	**Winter**	invierno *eenbee-yerno*

Clothes sizes

Men's Suits

British	36	38	40	42	44	46	48	50	
American	36	38	40	42	44	46	48	50	
Continental	46	48	50/52	54	56	58/60	62	64	

Men's Shirts

British	14	$14\frac{1}{2}$	15	$15\frac{1}{2}$	16	$16\frac{1}{2}$	17	$17\frac{1}{2}$
American	14	$14\frac{1}{2}$	15	$15\frac{1}{2}$	16	$16\frac{1}{2}$	17	$17\frac{1}{2}$
Continental	35	36/37	38	39/40	41	42/43	44	45

Men's Shoes

British	7	$7\frac{1}{2}$	8	$8\frac{1}{2}$	9	$9\frac{1}{2}$	10	$10\frac{1}{2}$	11
American	$7\frac{1}{2}$	8	$8\frac{1}{2}$	9	$9\frac{1}{2}$	10	$10\frac{1}{2}$	11	$11\frac{1}{2}$
Continental	41		42		43	45		45	

Women's Sizes

British	8	10	12	14	16	18	20	22
American	–	8	10	12	14	16	18	20
Continental	–	36	38	40	42	44	46	48

Women's Shoes

British	4	$4\frac{1}{2}$	5	6	$6\frac{1}{2}$	7	$7\frac{1}{2}$
American	$5\frac{1}{2}$	6	$6\frac{1}{2}$	$7\frac{1}{2}$	8	$8\frac{1}{2}$	9
Continental	36	37	38	39	40	41	41

Materials

brass	latón *laton*	**metal**	metálico/a *metaleeko/a*
glass	cristal *kreestal*	**wooden**	de madera *deh maderra*

Patterns and Fabrics

plain	liso/a *leeso/a*	**checked**	a cuadros *a kwadros*
printed	estampado/a *estampado/a*	**dotted**	de lunares *deh loonar-es*
striped	a rayas *a r-I-as*	**satin**	raso *raso*

Abbreviations

C	caliente	hot water (tap)
dcha	derecha	right
F	fría	cold water (tap)
IVA	impuesto del valor añadido	VAT
izq	izquierda	left
PVP	precio de venta al público	retail price
RENFE	Red Nacional de Ferrocarriles Españoles	Spanish Railway Company
SR	sin reserva	unreserved

Signs and public notices

abierto	open
agua potable	drinking water
aseos	toilets
centro ciudad	town centre
cerrado (por vacaciones)	closed (for holidays)
empujar	push
libre	vacant
no tocar	do not touch
ocupado	occupied
parada solicitada	request stop
peligro	danger
prohibido fumar	no smoking
prohibido el paso	no trespassing
prohibido pisar el césped	keep off the grass
recién pintado	wet paint
recoja el ticket	take a ticket
se prohibe la entrada	no entry/no admission
tirar	pull

WORDLIST

NB **f** indicates a feminine noun (*la*)
 m indicates a masculine noun (*el*)

A

a un/una
abdomen abdomen (m)
to be able poder
about aproximadamente/
 más o menos
above encima (de)
abroad al extranjero
abcess flemón (m)
accelerator acelerador (m)
to accept aceptar
accident accidente (m)
accommodation alojamien-
 to (m)
account cuenta (f)
ache dolor (m)
to ache doler
across a través (de)/al otro
 lado
activity actividad (f)
actor actor (m)
actress actriz (f)
adaptor adaptador (m)
address dirección (f)
adhesive tape cinta
 adhesiva (f)
admission entrada (f)
to admit admitir
adult adulto/a
advance (cash) anticipo (m)
advertisement anuncio (m)
aerial antena (f)
aeroplane avión (m)
Africa África
African africano/a
after después (de)
afternoon tarde (f)
aftershave loción de afeitar
 (f)
again otra vez
age edad (f)

agent agente/representante
 (m/f)
to agree estar de acuerdo
air conditioning aire
 acondicionado (m)
air-hostess azafata (f)
airline línea aérea (f)
airmail correo aéreo
airport aeropuerto (m)
alarm clock despertador
 (m)
alcohol alcohol (m)
all todo/a
allergic alérgico
alone solo/a
already ya
also también
although aunque
always siempre
amazing asombroso/a
ambulance ambulancia (f)
America Estados Unidos
American americano/a
amount cantidad (f)
amusing divertido/a
anaesthetic anestésico (m)
and y
angry enfadado/a
animal animal (m)
ankle tobillo (m)
annoyed enfadado/a
anorak anorak (m)
another otro/a
answer respuesta (f)
antibiotic antibiótico (m)
antidote antídoto (m)
antifreeze anticongelante
 (m)
antique antigüedad (f)
antiseptic antiséptico

137

anxious preocupado/a
any alguno/a; ninguno/a
apartment apartamento (m)
apology disculpa (f)
appendicitis apendicitis (f)
apple manzana (f)
appointment cita (f)
approximately aproxima-
   damente
apricot albaricoque (m)
architect arquitecto (m)
area área (f)
area code indicativo (m)
arm brazo (m)
armchair sillón (m)
around alrededor (de)
to arrive llegar
arrival llegada (f)
art arte (m)
art gallery galería de arte (f)
artichoke alcachofa (f)
artist artista (m/f)
ashtray cenicero (m)
to ask pedir/preguntar/
   invitar
asleep dormido/a
asparagus espárrago (m)
aspirin aspirina (f)
assistant ayudante (m/f)
asthma asma (f)
at a/en
atmosphere ambiente (m)
attack ataque (m)
attention atención (f)
attic ático (m)
attractive atractivo/a
aubergine berenjena (f)
aunt tía (f)
Australia Australia
Australian australiano/a
automatic automático/a
autumn otoño (m)
avocado aguacate (m)
away fuera/lejos (de)
awful horrible

B
baby bebé (m/f)
babysitter niñera (f)
back espalda (f)
backache dolor de espalda
   (m)

bacon tocino (m)
bad malo/a
bag bolso/a
baggage equipaje (m)
bakery panadería (f)
balcony balcón (m)
   (theatre) anfiteatro (m)
ball (dance) baile (m)
   (toy) pelota (f)
ball-point pen bolígrafo (m)
ban prohibición (f)
to ban prohibir
banana plátano (m)
band grupo (m)/orquesta
   (f)
bandage venda (f)
bank holiday día festivo (m)
banknote billete (m)
bar bar (m)/barra (f)
barbecue barbacoa (f)
barber's shop barbería (f)
basement sótano (m)
basket cesta (f)
basketball baloncesto (m)
bath baño (m)
bathing cap gorro de baño
   (m)
bathrobe albornoz (m)
bathroom cuarto de baño
   (m)
to bathe bañarse
battery (small) pila (f)
   (car) batería (f)
bay bahía (f)
to be ser/estar
beach playa (f)
bean judía (f)
beard barba (f)
beautiful hermoso/a
beauty salon salón de
   belleza (m)
because porque
bed cama (f)
bedding ropa de cama (f)
bedroom dormitorio (m)
bee abeja (f)
beef carne de vaca (f)
beer cerveza (f)
beetroot remolacha (f)
before antes
to begin empezar/comenzar
beginner principiante (m/f)

ehind atrás/detrás
ell timbre (m)/campana (f)
elow abajo/debajo (de)
elt cinturón (m)
ench banco (m)
end (in the road) curva (f)
est el/la mejor
etter mejor
etween entre
ib babero (m)
icycle bicicleta (f)
ig grande
ikini bikini (m)
ill cuenta (f)
in papelera (f)/cubo de basura (m)
inoculars prismáticos (m pl)
ird pájaro (m)
irthday cumpleaños (m)
iscuit galleta (f)
o bite morder/(insect) picar
ite picadura (f)
itter amargo/a
lack negro/a
lack pudding morcilla (f)
lanket manta (f)
leach lejía (f)
leeding hemorragia (f)
lind (for a window) persiana (f)
   (can't see) ciego/a
lister ampolla (f)
londe rubio/a
lood sangre (m)
 blood pressure tensión (f)
louse blusa (f)
lue azul
oat barco (m)/barca (f)
ody cuerpo (m)
oiled hervido/a
oiled egg (soft) huevo pasado por agua (m)
   (hard) huevo duro (m)
one hueso (m)
ook libro (m)
o book reservar
ooking office
   (theatre) taquilla (f)
   (Rail) despacho de billetes (m)

bookshop librería (f)
boot (shoe) bota (f)
   (car) capó (m)
border frontera (f)
boring aburrido/a
both ambos/los/las dos
bottle botella (f)
bottle-opener abridor de botellas (m)
box caja (f)
box office taquilla (f)
boy niño (m)/chico (m)
boyfriend amigo (m)/novio (m)
bra sujetador (m)
bracelet pulsera (f)
brakes frenos (mpl)
brake fluid líquido de frenos (m)
brand marca (f)
brandy coñac (m)
bread pan (m)
to break romper
breakdown (car) avería (f)
breakdown lorry grúa (f)
breakfast desayuno (m)
breast pecho (m)
to breathe respirar
bridge puente (f)
briefcase cartera (f)
to bring traer
Britain Gran Bretaña
British británico/a
broken roto/a
brochure folleto (m)
broom escoba (f)
brother hermano (m)
brother-in-law cuñado (m)
brown (colour) marrón
   (hair) castaño/a
   (tan) moreno/a
bruise contusión (f)/moradura (f)
brush cepillo (m)
bucket cubo (m)
building edificio (m)
bulb bombilla (f)
bull toro (m)
bullfight corrida (f)
bullfighter torero (m)
bullring plaza de toros (f)
bump golpe (m)

bumper parachoques (m)
bunch (of flowers) ramo (m)
bungalow bungalow (m)
bunk litera (f)
burglar ladrón (m)
burglary robo (m)
burn quemadura (f)
to burn quemar
bus autobús (m)
  bus station estación de autobuses (f)
  bus stop parada (f)
but pero
business negocio (m)
  business trip viaje de negocios (m)
butane butano (m)
butcher's shop carnicería (f)
butter mantequilla (f)
button botón (m)
to buy comprar

C

cab taxi (m)
cabbage repollo (m)
cafe cafetería (f)
cake pastel (m)
  cake shop pastelería (f)
calendar calendario (m)
call (telephone) llamada (f)
to call (shout) llamar
  (telephone) telefonear
camera cámara fotográfica (f)
camp campamento (m)
to camp acampar/hacer camping
camp site camping (m)
can (to be able) poder
can lata (f)
Canada Canadá
Canadian canadiense
to cancel cancelar/anular
candy caramelo (m)
can opener abrelatas (m)
car coche (m)
  car hire alquiler de coches (m)
  car park parking (m)/ aparcamiento (m)
  car wash lavado de coches (m)
caravan caravana (f)
carburettor carburador (m)
card (visiting) tarjeta (f)
  (postcard) postal (f)
  (membership) carnet (m)
cardigan chaqueta de punto (f)
careful! ¡cuidado!
carriage vagón m/coche (m)
carrot zanahoria (f)
to carry llevar
carton (of cigarettes) cartón (de cigarrillos) (m)
case (for jewels, glasses) estuche (m)
  (suitcase) maleta (f)
cash dinero (m)
to cash cobrar
cash desk caja (f)
cashier cajero/a
cassette cassette (m)/cinta (f)
castanets castañuelas (fpl)
castle castillo (m)
cat gato (m)
cathedral catedral (f)
cauliflower coliflor (f)
celery apio (m)
cellar bodega (f)
central heating calefacción central (f)
centre centro (m)
century siglo (m)
ceramics cerámica (f)
chain cadena (f)
chair silla (f)
chalet chalet (m)
champagne (French) champán (m)
  (Spanish) cava (m)
change cambio (m)
to change cambiar
changing room probador (m)
chapel capilla (f)
to charge cobrar
charter flight vuelo charter (m)

heap barato/a
check revisar/comprobar
check in (**hotel**) inscribirse
(**airport**) presentarse
heck up (**medical**) reconocimiento (m)
heers! ¡salud!
heerio! ¡hasta luego!
heese queso (m)
hemist's farmacia (f)
heque cheque (m)
hequebook talonario (m)
heque card tarjeta de banco (f)
herry cereza (f)
hest pecho (m)
hewing gum chicle (m)
hicken pollo (m)
chicken breast pechuga de pollo (f)
hick pea garbanzo (m)
hild niño/a
hina porcelana (f)
hina China
hinese chino/a
hips patatas fritas (fpl)
hlorine cloro (m)
hocolate chocolate (m)
hop chuleta (f)
hristmas Navidad (f)
hurch iglesia (f)
der sidra (f)
gar puro (m)
garette cigarrillo (m)
cigarette lighter encendedor (m)
cigarette paper papel de fumar (m)
nema cine (m)
rcle (**theatre**) anfiteatro (m)
(**shape**) círculo (m)
rcus circo (m)
ty ciudad (f)
vil servant funcionario/a
aim reclamación (f)
claim reclamar
ass clase (f)
ean limpio/a
clean limpiar

client cliente (m/f)
climate clima (m)
clinic clínica (f)
cloakroom guardarropa (m)
clock (**wall**) reloj (m)
(**alarm**) despertador (m)
to close cerrar
closed cerrado/a
cloth tela (f)
clothes ropa (f)
cloud nube (f)
club club (m)
clutch (**car**) embrague (m)
coach autocar (m)
coast costa (f)
coat abrigo (m)
cocoa cacao (m)
coconut coco (m)
code código (m)
area code prefijo (m)
coffee café (m)
(**black**) café solo (m)
(**white**) café con leche (m)
coin moneda (f)
cold frío (m)
to be cold (**person**) tener frío
(**weather**) hacer frío
to have a cold estar resfriado/a
collar cuello (m)
colour color (m)
comb peine (m)
to come venir
comedy comedia (f)
comfortable cómodo/a
comic (**magazine**) tebeo (m)
Common Market Mercado Común (m)
compact disc disco compacto (m)
company compañía (f)/ empresa (f)
to complain quejarse
complaint queja (f)
computer ordenador (m)
concert concierto (m)

concussion conmoción cerebral (f)
condom preservativo (m)
conductor (bus) cobrador (m)
confectioner's confitería (f)
congratulations felicidades (f pl)
connection (transport) conexión (f)/transbordo (m)
constipated estreñido/a
consulate consulado (m)
contact lens lente de contacto (f)
contagious contagioso/a
contraceptive anticonceptivo (m)
control control (m)
controller controlador (m)
cooker cocina (f)
cool fresco/a
cork corcho (m)
corkscrew sacacorchos (m)
corn maíz (m)
corner esquina (f)
cosmetics cosméticos (mpl)
cost precio (m)
to cost costar
costume traje (m)
cot cuna (f)
cottage chalet (m)
cottage cheese requesón (m)
cotton algodón (m)
cotton wool algodón hidrófilo (m)
cough tos (f)
to cough toser
counter (shop) mostrador (m)
country país (m)
countryside campo (m)
couple pareja (f)
courgette calabacín (m)
course (meal) plato (m)
(golf) campo (m)
cousin primo/a
crab cangrejo (m)
crafts artesanía (f)
cramp calambre (m)
crash choque (m)
142   **crash course** curso

intensivo (m)
crash helmet casco (m)
cream nata (f)
credit card tarjeta de crédito (f)
crisps patatas fritas (f pl)
crossing cruce (m)
(pedestrian) paso de peatones (m)
crossroads cruce (m)
cruise crucero (m)
cucumber pepino (m)
cuisine cocina (f)
cup taza (f)
to cure curar
currency moneda (f)
current corriente (f)
current account cuenta corriente (f)
cushion cojín (m)
custard natilla (f)
customs aduana (f)
customer cliente (m/f)
cut corte (m)
(wound) herida (f)
to cut cortar
cutlery cubiertos (m pl)
cycling ciclismo (m)
cyclist ciclista (m/f)

D
daily diariamente
dairy lechería (f)
dance baile (m)
to dance bailar
dance hall sala de baile (f)
danger peligro (m)
dangerous peligroso/a
dark oscuro/a
date (calendar) fecha (f)
(fruit) dátil (m)
daughter hija (f)
day día (m)
deaf sordo/a
dear querido/a
dear Sir/Madam (letter) estimado/a señor/señora
deck chair hamaca (f)
deep profundo/a
to dehydrate deshidratar
delay retraso (m)

elicate   delicado/a
elicatessen   mantequería (f)
elivery service   servicio a domicilio (m)
entist   dentista (m/f)
enture   dentadura postiza (f)
eodorant   desodorante (m)
epartment   departamento (m)
epartment store   grandes almacenes (mpl)
eposit   depósito (m)
deposit (bank)   ingresar
essert   postre (m)
etergent   detergente (m)
etour   desvío (m)
iabetes   diabetes (f)
iabetic   diabético/a
dial   marcar
ialling tone   señal de marcar (f)
iarrhoea   diarrea (f)
ictionary   diccionario (m)
iesel oil   gasoil (m)
iet   régimen (m)
ifficult   difícil
ining-car   coche restaurante (m)
ining-room   comedor (m)
inner   cena (f)
dinner jacket   esmoquin (m)
irect   directo/a
irection   dirección (f)
irections   instrucciones (f pl)
irectory   listín (m)
irty   sucio/a
isabled   minusválido/a
iscount   descuento (m)
ish   plato (m)
ishwasher   lavaplatos (m)
isinfectant   desinfectante (m)
istance   distancia (f)
disturb   molestar
iversion   desvío (m)
ivorced   divorciado/a
izzy   mareado/a
octor   médico

dog   perro (m)
do-it-yourself   bricolaje (m)
doll   muñeca (f)
dollar   dólar (m)
door   puerta (f)
doorbell   timbre (m)
double   doble
double bed   cama de matrimonio (f)/cama doble (f)
double room   habitación doble (f)
down   abajo
downstairs   abajo
dozen   docena (f)
drawer   cajón (m)
dress   vestido (m)
dressing gown   bata (f)
(evening) dress   traje de noche (m)
drier   secador (m)
drink   bebida (f)
to drink   beber
drinking water   agua potable (f)
to drive   conducir
driving licence   permiso de conducir (m)
drug   medicamento (m)
drugs   drogas (f pl)
drunk   borracho/a
dry   seco/a
to dry clean   limpiar en seco
dry cleaner's   tintorería (f)
dual carriageway   carretera de doble carril (f)
dummy (baby)   chupete (m)
during   durante
duty (tax)   impuestos (m pl)
duty free   libre de impuestos

E
each   cada
ear   oreja (f)
earache   dolor de oído (m)
early   temprano/pronto
earring   pendiente (m)
easy   fácil
to eat   comer
eczema   eczema (m)
egg   huevo (m)

elbow codo (m)
electric eléctrico/a
electrician electricista (m/f)
electricity electricidad (f)
embassy embajada (f)
emergency emergencia (f)/
    urgencia (f)
  emergency exit salida de
    emergencia (f)
employer empresario/a
empty vacío/a
end final (f)
engine motor (m)
England Inglaterra
English inglés/esa
to enjoy oneself divertirse
enjoyable divertido/a
enough bastante
to enrol
    (school) matricularse
entertaining entretenido/a
entrance entrada (f)
envelope sobre (f)
environment ambiente (m)
epilepsy epilepsia (f)
equipment equipo (m)
error error (m)
escalator escalera mecánica
    (f)
evening (early) tarde (f)
        (late) noche (f)
exactly exactamente
exchange rate cambio (m)
excursion excursión (f)
excuse me! ¡oiga!
exercise ejercicio (m)
exhaust pipe tubo de escape
    (m)
exhibition exposición (f)
exit salida (f)
expenses gastos (m pl)
expensive caro/a
to export exportar
express (delivery) urgente
        (train) rápido (m)
extension (telephone)
    extensión (f)
eye ojo (m)
  eye drops gotas para los
    ojos (fpl)
  eye shadow sombra de
    ojos (la)

eye specialist oculista (m
    f)
eye witness testigo (m/f)

F
fabric tejido (m)
face cara (f)
factory fábrica (f)
to faint desmayarse
fair (hair) rubio/a
    (funfair) feria (f)/
    parque de atracciones
    (m)
fall caída (f)
to fall caerse
family familia (f)
fan (hand) abanico (m)
    (electric) ventilador (m
    (sports) aficionado/a
fanbelt correa de ventilador
    (f)
fancy dress disfraz (m)
far lejos
fare precio de billete (m)
farm granja (f)
fashion moda (f)
fast rápido/a
to fasten abrochar
fat (meat) grasa (f)
    (person) gordo/a
father padre (m)
fault (person) culpa (f)
    (object) defecto (m)
fee precio (m)
feeding bottle biberón (m)
to feel (ill) sentirse (mal)
    (touch) tocar
ferry transbordador (m)
fever fiebre (f)
few pocos/as
field campo (m)
fig higo (m)
to fill llenar
filling (tooth) empaste (m)
filling station gasolinera (f)
film (cinema) película (f)
    (photo) rollo (m)
filter filtro (m)
fine! ¡muy bien!
finger dedo (m)
to finish terminar
fire fuego (m)

(gas or electric) estufa (f)
fire alarm alarma de incendios (f)
fire brigade bomberos (m pl)
fire escape escalera de incendios (f)
fire extinguisher extintor (m)
fireplace chimenea (f)
fireproof incombustible
firm (business) empresa (f)
first aid primeros auxilios (m pl)
first name nombre de pila (m)
fish pescado (m)
to fish pescar
fishbone espina (f)
fishmonger's pescadería (f)
fitting room probador (m)
flashlight linterna (f)
flat llano/a/plano/a
(battery) batería descargada (f)
(apartment) piso (m)
flat tyre pinchazo (m)
flight vuelo (m)
flip-flops chancletas (f)
floor (ground) suelo (m)
(in building) piso (m)
florist's floristería (f)
flour harina (f)
flower flor (f)
flu gripe (f)
fly mosca (f)
to fly volar
fog niebla (f)
folding plegable
food comida (f)
food poisoning intoxicación alimenticia (f)
foot pie (m)
football fútbol (m)
footpath camino (m)
for por/para
forbidden prohibido/a
forecast
(weather) pronóstico del tiempo (m)
forehead frente (f)

foreign extranjero/a
forest bosque (m)
fork tenedor (m)
form (shape) forma (f)
(document) ficha (f)
fortnight quincena (f)
fountain fuente (f)
fracture fractura (f)
fragile frágil
France Francia
free (vacant) libre
(no charge) gratis
French francés/esa
frequent frecuente
fresh fresco/a
fridge nevera (f)/frigorífico (m)
fried frito/a
friend amigo/a
friendly simpático/a
from de/desde
front parte delantera (f)
frontier frontera (f)
frozen congelado/a
fruit fruta (f)
fruit machine máquina tragaperras (f)
fruit juice zumo de fruta (m)/jugo (m)
fruit salad macedonia de frutas (f)
fruit shop frutería (f)
to fry freír
frying pan sartén (f)
full lleno/a
full board pensión completa (f)
full insurance seguro a todo riesgo (m)
funfair feria (f)/parque de attracciones (m)
funny (comic) divertido/a
(strange) extraño/a
furnished amueblado/a
furniture muebles (m pl)
further más lejos/más allá
fuse fusible (m)
fuse box caja de fusibles (f)

G
game juego (m)

garage garaje (m)
garden jardín (m)
garlic ajo (m)
gas gas (m)
gate puerta (f)
gear (car) marcha (f)
gearbox caja de velocidades
    (f)
general general
gentleman caballero (m)
gents caballeros (m pl)
Germany Alemania
German alemán/ana
to get obtener/coger
to get up levantarse
gift regalo (m)
gin ginebra (f)
girl niña (f)/chica (f)
girlfriend amiga (f)/novia
    (f)
to give dar
glad contento/a
glass vaso (m)
glasses gafas (f pl)
glove guante (m)
to go ir/irse
to go out salir
gold oro (m)
golf golf (m)
    golf club (group) club de
        golf (m)
    (stick) palo de golf (m)
    golf course campo de golf
        (m)
good bueno/a
    good afternoon buenas
        tardes (f pl)
    goodbye adiós
    good evening buenas
        tardes (f pl)/buenas
        noches (f pl)
    good morning buenos
        días (m pl)
    good night buenas
        noches (f pl)
goods artículos (m pl)
government gobierno (m)
gram gramo (m)
grandchild nieto/a
grandfather abuelo (m)
grandmother abuela (f)

grandparents abuelos (m p
grape uva (f)
grapefruit pomelo (m)
gravy salsa (f)
greasy grasiento/a
Greece Grecia
Greek griego/a
green verde
green bean judía verde (f)
greengrocer's verdulería (f
greetings recuerdos (m pl)/
    saludos (m pl)
grey gris
grill parrilla (f)
grilled a la parrilla/a la
    plancha
grocer's tienda de
    comestibles (f)
ground suelo (m)
    ground floor planta baja
        (f)
group grupo (m)
guest invitado/a
guest-house casa de
    huéspedes (f)
guide guía (f/m)
    guidebook guía turística
        (f)
    guided tour visita
        acompañada (f)
guitar guitarra (f)
gum (teeth) encía (f)
    (chewing) chicle (m)

H
hair pelo (f)
    hairbrush cepillo para el
        pelo (m)
    hairdresser's peluquería
        (f)
    hair dryer secador (m)
    hairspray laca (f)
half mitad (f)
    half board media pensió
        (f)
ham jamón (m)
hamburger hamburguesa
    (f)
hammer martillo (m)
hand mano (f)

handkerchief pañuelo (m)
handbag bolso (m)
handmade hecho/a a mano
hanger percha (f)
happy feliz
hard duro/a
  hard boiled egg huevo duro (m)
hat sombrero (m)
to have tener
hay fever fiebre del heno (f)
head cabeza (f)
headache dolor de cabeza (m)
health salud (f)
heart corazón (m)
  heart attack ataque cardiaco (m)/infarto (m)
heat calor (m)
heater calentador (m)
heating calefacción (f)
hello! ¡hola!
help! ¡socorro!
help ayuda (f)
to help ayudar
here aquí
hi-fi estéreo (m)
high alto/a
  high-chair silla para niño (f)
  high street calle principal (f)
to hire alquilar
to hitch-hike hacer autostop
hitch-hiking autostop (m)
holiday fiesta (f)
holiday resort centro turístico (m)
holidays vacaciones (f pl)
home casa (f)
  home address dirección (f)
honey miel (f)
honeymoon luna de miel (f)
horse caballo (m)
  horse riding montar a caballo
hospital hospital (m)
hostel hostal (m)

youth hostel albergue juvenil (m)
hot caliente
to be hot (person) tener calor
      (weather) hacer calor
hotel hotel (m)
hour hora (f)
house casa (f)
housewife ama de casa (f)
how? ¿cómo?
  how big? ¿De qué tamaño?
  how far? ¿A qué distancia?
  how long? ¿Cuánto tiempo?
  how much? ¿Cuánto?
to be hungry tener hambre
hurry prisa (f)
to be in a hurry tener prisa
hurry up! ¡de prisa!
to hurt doler
husband marido (m)

I
ice hielo (m)
  ice cream helado (m)
  ice cube cubito de hielo (m)
  ice skating patinaje sobre hielo (m)
idea idea (f)
identity card carnet de identidad (m)
ill enfermo/a
illegal ilegal
illness enfermedad (f)
immediately inmediatamente
to import importar
important importante
impossible imposible
in en
included incluído/a
India India
Indian indio/a
indigestion indigestión (f)

indoor interior (m)
  indoor pool piscina cubierta (f)
industry industria (f)
infection infección (f)
infectious contagioso/a
information información (f)
injection inyección (f)
injury herida (f)
inquiries información (f)
insect bite picadura de insecto (f)
inside dentro
insurance seguro (m)
  third party insurance seguro contra terceros (m)
  comprehensive insurance seguro a todo riesgo
  insurance company companía de seguros (f)
interesting interesante
international internacional
interpreter intérprete (m/f)
intersection cruce (m)
interval descanso (m)
to invest invertir
invitation invitación (f)
to invite invitar
invoice factura (f)
Ireland Irlanda
Irish irlandés/esa
iron (utensil) plancha (f)
  (metal) hierro (m)
to iron planchar
island isla (f)
Italy Italia
Italian italiano/a
itinerary itinerario (m)

J
jacket chaqueta (f)
jail cárcel (f)
jam mermelada (f)
jar tarro (m)
jeans pantalones vaqueros (m pl)
jersey jersey (m)
148   **jewellery** joyas (fpl)

job trabajo (m)
juice jugo/zumo (m)
junction cruce (f)

K
key llave (f)
to keep guardar
kind (nice) amable/bueno/a
  (type) tipo (m)
kitchen cocina (f)
knee rodilla (f)
knickers bragas (f pl)
knife cuchillo (m)
to knock (on a door) llama
to know (facts) saber
  (people) conocer

L
lace (shoe) cordón (m)
  (fabric) puntilla (f)
ladder escalera de mano (f)
lady señora (f)
ladies (toilets) servicios señoras (mpl)
lager cerveza (f)
lake lago (m)
lamb cordero (m)
lamp (table) lámpara (f)
  (street) farol (m)
landscape paisaje (m)
lane (country) camino (m)
  (motorway) carril (m)
language lenguaje (m)/ idioma (m)/lengua (f)
large grande
last último/a
  last night anoche
late (time) tarde
  (delayed) retrasado/a
later más tarde
launderette lavandería (automática) (f)
lavatory servicios (m pl)
law ley (f)
lawyer abogado (m)
laxative laxante (m)
lead (metal) plomo (m)
leak gotera (f)
to leak gotear
lean (meat) magro/sin gras
to learn aprender
leather cuero (m)

o **leave** irse/marcharse/salir	**local** local/cercano/a
eft izquierda (f)	**lock** cerradura (f)
eg pierna (f)	**long** largo/a
eisure tiempo libre (m)	**loo** servicio (m)
emon limón (m)	to **look** mirar
emonade limonada (f)/ gaseosa (f)	to **look after** cuidar
ens lente (f)	to **look for** buscar
(**contact**) lente de contacto	**lorry** camión (m)
entil lenteja (f)	to **lose** perder
ess menos	**lost property** objetos perdidos (m pl)
esson lección (f)/clase (f)	**lounge** salón (m)
etter carta (f)	**love** amor (m)
ettuce lechuga (f)	to **fall in love** enamorarse
brary biblioteca (f)	(**end of letter**) un abrazo (m)
cence licencia (f)/permiso (m)	to **love** querer
driving licence carnet de conducir (m)	**lovely** bonito/a
o **lie down** acostarse	**luggage** equipaje (m)
febelt cinturón salvavidas (m)	**lunch** comida (f)/almuerzo (m)
feboat bote salvavidas (m)	**lunchtime** mediodía (m)/ hora de comer (f)
feguard socorrista (m/f)	**lung** pulmón (m)
fe jacket chaleco salvavidas (m)	**M**
ft ascensor (m)	**machine** máquina (f)
ght (**lamp**) lámpara (f)	**madam** señora (f)
(**colour**) claro/a	**magazine** revista (f)
light bulb bombilla (f)	**maid** camarera (f)
o **light** encender	**mail** correo (m)
ghter encendedor (m)	**main** principal
o **like** gustar	**main road** carretera general (f)
me lima (f)	to **make** hacer
p labio (m)	**make up** maquillaje (m)
pstick lápiz de labios (m)	**man** hombre (m)
quid líquido (m)	**manager** director/a
o **listen** oir/escuchar	**manicure** manicura (f)
tre litro (m)	**many** muchos/as
tter basura (f)	**map** (**road**) mapa (m)
tter-bin papelera (f)	(**town**) plano (m)
ttle pequeño/a	**margarine** margarina (f)
a little un poco	**market** mercado (m)
o **live** vivir	**marmalade** mermelada (f)
ver hígado (m)	**married** casado/a
ving room cuarto de estar (m)	**mascara** rimel (m)
oaf pan (m)	**match** (**for lighting**) cerilla (f)
oaf (**long**) barra (f)	(**sport**) partido (m)
obster langosta (f)	**material** (**cloth**) tela (f)
	mattress colchón (m)

maybe quizás
mayonnaise mayonesa (f)
meal comida (f)
to mean querer decir
measles sarampión (m)
to measure medir
  made to measure hecho/a a medida
measurement medida (f)
meat carne (f)
mechanic mecánico (m/f)
medicine medicina (f)
to meet encontrar
meeting reunión (f)
melon melón (m)
member socio/a
to mend arreglar/reparar
menu menú (m)
  à la carte menu carta (f)
message recado (m)
meter contador (m)
metre metro (m)
midday mediodía (m)
middle medio (m)
midnight medianoche (f)
mild suave
mile milla (f)
mileage kilometraje (m)
milk leche (f)
  milk chocolate chocolate con leche (m)
  milkshake batido (m)
mince carne picada (f)
mineral water agua mineral (f)
minimum mínimo/a
minor menor
  (road) carretera secundaria (f)
mint menta (f)
minute minuto (m)
miss (title) señorita (f)
to miss (train) perder
missing desaparecido/a
mistake error (m)
mistaken equivocado/a
mixed salad ensalada mixta (f)
moisturizing cream crema hidratante (f)
moment momento (m)
monastery monasterio (m)
money dinero (m)

month mes (m)
more más
morning mañana (f)
mosquito mosquito (m)
mosquito bite picadura de mosquito (f)
most la mayoría
mother madre (f)
motor motor (m)
  motorbike moto (f)
  motorboat lancha motora (f)
  motorist automovilista (m/f)
motorway autopista (f)
mountain montaña (f)
moustache bigote (m)
mouth boca (f)
to move mover/
  (house) cambiarse de (casa)
movie película (f)
Mr señor (m)
Mrs señora (f)
much mucho
mug tazón (m)
muscle músculo (m)
museum museo (m)
mushroom champiñón (m)
music música (f)
musical comedia musical (f)
must (to have to) tener que
mustard mostaza (f)

N
nail (metal) clavo (m)
  (finger) uña (f)
  nail polish esmalte (m)
  nail polish remover quitaesmalte (de uñas) (m)
name nombre (m)
  surname apellido (m)
napkin servilleta (f)
nappy pañal (m)
nationality estrecho/a
narrow nacionalidad (f)
natural natural
near cerca
necessary necesario/a
neck cuello (m)
necklace collar (m)
to need necesitar

needle   aguja (f)
neighbour   vecino/a
nephew   sobrino (m)
nervous   nervioso/a
never   nunca
new   nuevo/a
news   noticias (fpl)
newspaper   periódico (m)
New Zealand   Nueva
    Zelanda
next (in queue)   siguiente
    (week etc)   próximo/a
next to   al lado de
nice (thing)   bonito/a
    (person)   simpático/a
niece   sobrina (f)
night   noche (f)
nightclub   club(m)/sala de
    fiestas(f)
nightdress   camisón (m)
noise   ruido (m)
non-alcoholic (drink)   sin
    alcohol
non-stop (train)   directo/a
normal   normal
north   norte (m)
Northern Ireland   Irlanda
    del Norte
nose   nariz (f)
nosebleed   hemorragia nasal
    (f)
note (money)   billete (m)
    (message)   recado (m)
nothing   nada
now   ahora
nuisance   molestia (f)
number   número (m)
    number plate   matrícula
    (f)
nurse   enfermero/a
nut   nuez (f)

O
object   objeto (m)
occupation   profesión (f)
off (food)   malo/a
office   oficina (f)
oil   aceite (m)
OK   de acuerdo/vale
old   viejo/a
olive   oliva (f)/aceituna (f)

olive oil   aceite de oliva
    (m)
omelette   tortilla (f)
on   sobre/en
one-way (street)   dirección
    única (f)
    (ticket)   sencillo
onion   cebolla (f)
only   solamente
open   abierto/a
to open   abrir
open-air   al aire libre
opera   ópera (f)
operation   operación (f)
operator   telefonista (m/f)
opposite (place)   enfrente
    (de)
optician   óptico (m)
or   o
orange   naranja (f)
    orange juice   zumo de
    naranja (m)
orangeade   naranjada (f)
orchestra   orquesta (f)
to order   pedir
other   otro/a
out of order   estropeado/a
outside   fuera
oven   horno (m)
overdone   demasiado hecho/
    a
overnight   por la noche
    to stay overnight   pasar la
    noche
overseas   extranjero (m)
to overtake   adelantar
to owe   deber
owner   dueño/a

P
package holiday   viaje
    organizado (m)
packet   paquete (m)
paddle boat   patín (m)
pain   dolor (m)
painkiller   calmante (m)/
    analgésico (m)
painting   cuadro (m)
pair (objects)   par (m)
    (people)   pareja (f)
palace   palacio (m)
panties   bragas (f pl)

paper papel (m)
parcel paquete (m)
pardon? ¿cómo?
parents padres (m pl)
park parque
to park aparcar
parking aparcamiento (m)
   parking
      meter parquímetro (m)
   parking ticket multa (f)
part parte (f)
   (car) pieza (f)
partner (social) compañero/
   a
      (business) socio/a
party fiesta (f)
passenger pasajero/a
passport pasaporte (m)
path camino (m)
patient paciente (m/f)
to pay pagar
to pay in (at a
   bank) ingresar
pea guisante (m)
peach melocotón (m)
peanut cacahuete (m)
pear pera (f)
pedestrian peatón (m/f)
   pedestrian crossing paso
   de peatones (m)
peg (clothes) pinza (f)
pen pluma (f)
pencil lápiz (m)
penicillin penicilina (f)
penis pene (m)
pensioner pensionista (m/f)/
   jubilado/a
people gente (f)
pepper pimienta (f)
performance
   (theatre) función (f)
   (cinema) sesión (f)
perfume perfume (m)
perhaps quizás
period periodo (m)
   (menstrual) regla (f)
perm permanente (f)
permit permiso (m)
person persona (f)
petrol gasolina (f)
   petrol pump surtidor de
      gasolina (m)

petrol station gasolinera
   (f)
   petrol tank depósito de
      gasolina (m)
pharmacy farmacia (f)
phone teléfono (m)
to phone llamar por
   teléfono
photo foto (f)
phrase book libro de frases
   (m)
to pick up buscar/recoger
picnic merienda (f)
picture cuadro (m)/imagen
   (f)
piece trozo (m)
pig cerdo (m)
pill píldora (f)
pillow almohada (f)
pin alfiler (m)
pineapple piña (f)
pink rosa
pipe (water) tubería (f)
   (tobacco) pipa (f)
place lugar (m)
plan plan (m)
   (map) plano (m)
plane avión (m)
plant planta (f)
plastic plástico (m)
plate plato (m)
platform andén (m)/vía (f)
play (theatre) obra (f)
to play (game) jugar
   (instrument) tocar
playground zona de juegos
   infantiles (f)
pleasant agradable
please por favor
plug (sink) tapón (m)
   (electrical) enchufe (m)
to plug in enchufar
plum ciruela (f)
plumber fontanero/a
pocket bolsillo (m)
police policía (f)
policeman policía (m)
policewoman mujer policía
   (f)
pool (swimming) piscina (f)
poor pobre
popular popular

port (harbour) puerto (m)
    (drink) vino de Oporto (m)
pork cerdo (m)
porter (attendant) mozo (m)
    (doorman) portero (m)
portion porción (f)
Portugal Portugal
Portuguese portugués/esa
possible posible
post correo (m)
to post enviar/mandar/echar
  postage stamp sello (m)
  post box buzón (f)
  postcard tarjeta postal (f)
  post code código postal (m)
  post man cartero (m)
poster cartel (m)
post office correos (m pl)
potato patata (f)
pottery (objects) cerámica (f)
powder polvo (m)
pram cochecito de niño (m)
prawn gamba (f)
precaution precaución (f)
to prefer preferir
pregnant embarazada
to prepare preparar
prescription receta (f)
present (gift) regalo (m)
press (newspapers) prensa (f)
to press (button) empujar
to press (trousers) planchar
pretty bonito/a
price precio (m)
private (personal) privado/a/personal
  (lesson etc) particular
prize premio (m)
probably probablemente
problem problema (m)
profession profesión (f)
programme programa (m)
prohibited prohibido/a
property propiedad (f)

proprietor propietario(m)/dueño (m)
to prosecute proseguir
to protect proteger
pub taberna (f)/pub (m)
public público (m)
public transport servicio de transportes públicos (m)
to pull tirar
pullover jersey (m)
punch (drink) ponche (m)
  (blow) golpe (m)
puncture pinchazo (m)
purse monedero (m)
to push empujar
to put poner
pyjamas pijama (m)

Q
quality calidad (f)
quantity cantidad (f)
quarter cuarto (m)
queasy mareado/a
question pregunta (f)
queue cola (f)
to queue hacer cola
quick rápido/a
quickly rápidamente
quiet silencioso/a

R
rabbit conejo (m)
race (sport) carrera (f)
racket raqueta (f)
radiator radiador (m)
radio radio (f)
railway ferrocarril (m)
rain lluvia (f)
to rain llover
raincoat impermeable (m)
rape violación (f)
to rape violar
rare (meat) poco/a hecho/a
  (unusual) raro/a
rash erupción (f)
raspberry frambuesa (f)
raw (uncooked) crudo/a
razor navaja (f)
  safety razor maquinilla de afeitar (f)
  electric razor máquina de afeitar eléctrica (f)

razor blade hoja de afeitar (f)
to reach (arrive at) llegar
to read leer
ready preparado/a/listo/a
real real/verdadero/a
receipt recibo (m)/ticket (m)
receive recibir
recent reciente
reception (hotel) recepción (f)
receptionist recepcionista (m/f)
to recommend recomendar
record (music) disco (m)
  record-player tocadiscos (m)
recorded delivery certificado (m)
to recover recuperar
red rojo/a
refrigerator frigorífico(m)/ nevera (f)
refund reembolso (m)
to refuse negar
regular regular
relative (family) pariente/a
to relax relajar/descansar
to remain quedarse
to remember recordar/ acordarse
to remove sacar/quitar
rent alquiler (m)
to rent alquilar
to repair reparar/arreglar
to repeat repetir
to replace sustituir
to represent representar
representative represen- tante (m/f)
request demanda (f)
to request pedir
to reserve reservar
resort centro turístico (m)
responsible responsable
rest descanso (m)
to rest descansar
restaurant restaurante (m)
result resultado (m)
retired (person) jubilado/a
return (ticket) un billete de ida y vuelta

to return (go back) volver
  (money) devolver
reverse (gear) marcha atrás (f)
rib costilla (f)
rice arroz (m)
rich rico/a
to ride (a horse) montar (a caballo)
right (direction) derecha (f)
to be right tener razón
rights derechos (m pl)
ring (jewellery) anillo (m)
ring road carretera de circunvalación (f)
to ring (phone) llamar
  (bell) sonar
rink pista (f)
  ice rink pista de hielo (f)
ripe maduro/a
risk riesgo (m)
river río (m)
road camino (m)/carretera (f)
  road sign señal de tráfico (f)
roadworks obras (f pl)
roast asado/a
to rob robar
roll (bread) panecillo (m)
roof tejado (m)
  roof rack baca (f)
room (house) cuarto (m)
  (hotel) habitación (f)
rope cuerda (f)
round redondo/a
route ruta (f)
row (theatre) fila (f)
rubbish basura (f)
rucksack mochila (f)
rude grosero/a
ruins ruinas (f pl)
rules reglamento (m)
to run correr

S
sad triste
safe (for money) caja fuerte (f)
  (no danger) seguro/a
safety pin imperdible (m)
to sail navegar

sailing boat   velero (m)
salad   ensalada (f)
   salad cream   mayonesa (f)
   salad dressing   vinagreta (f)
salami   salchichón (m)
sale   venta (f)/rebajas (f pl)
   for sale   se vende
salesperson   dependiente/a
salmon   salmón (m)
salt   sal (f)
sand   arena (f)
sandal   sandalia (f)
sandwich   sandwich (m)/ bocadillo (m)
sanitary towel   compresa (f)
sardine   sardina (f)
sauce   salsa (f)
saucepan   cacerola (f)
saucer   platito (m)
sausage   salchicha (f)
scarf   pañuelo (m)
   (woollen)   bufanda (f)
scenery   paisaje (m)
school   escuela (f)
scissors   tijeras (f pl)
Scotland   Escocia
Scottish   escocés/esa
screwdriver   destornillador (m)
sea   mar (m/f)
   sea food   mariscos (m pl)
   sea front   paseo marítimo (m)
seaside   costa (f)
season   temporada (f)
   season ticket   abono (m)
seasoning   condimento (m)
seat   asiento (m)
   seat belt   cinturón de seguridad (m)
second   segundo/a
secretary   secretario/a
section   sección (f)
to see   ver
see you later!   ¡hasta luego!
self-service   autoservicio (m)
to sell   vender
to send   enviar
to serve   servir
service   servicio (m)
serviette   servilleta (f)

to sew   coser
shade   sombra (f)
shampoo   champú (m)
sharp   agudo/a
to shave   afeitarse
shaver   maquinilla de afeitar (f)
shaving cream   crema de afeitar (f)
sheet (bed)   sábana (f)
   (of paper)   hoja (f)
shellfish   mariscos (m pl)
sherry   jerez (m)
ship   barco (m)
shirt   camisa (f)
shoe   zapato (m)
   shoelace   cordón de zapatos (m)
   shoe repairer's   zapatero (m)
   shoe shop   zapatería (f)
shop   tienda (f)
   shop assistant   dependiente/a
shopping   compras (f pl)
   to go shopping   ir de compras
   shopping centre   centro comercial (m)
short   corto/a
shorts   pantalones cortos (m pl)
short-sighted   miope
show   espectáculo (m)
to show   mostrar
shower   ducha (f)
shut   cerrado/a
sick (ill)   enfermo/a
   (sea/air)   mareado/a
sickness   enfermedad (f)
side effects   efectos secundarios (m pl)
sightseeing   visita turística (f)
sign   señal (f)
to sign   firmar
signature   firma (f)
silk   seda (f)
silly   tonto/a
silver   plata (f)
since   desde
singer   cantante (m/f)

155

single (bed, room) individual
  (ticket) sencillo/a
  (person) soltero/a
sink (bathroom) lavabo (m)
sir señor (m)
sister hermana (f)
size (clothes) talla (f)
  (shoes) número (m)
  (object) tamaño (m)
to skate patinar
skating patinaje (m)
  skating rink pista de patinaje (f)
ski esquí (m)
to ski esquiar
ski lift telesquí(m)/telesilla (m)
skin piel (f)
skirt falda (f)
to sleep dormir
sleeping bag saco de dormir (m)
sleeping car coche cama (m)
slide (photo) diapositiva (f)
slipper zapatilla (f)
slow despacio/lento/a
small pequeño/a
  small change dinero suelto (m)
to smoke fumar
smoker fumador/a
snack tapa (f)
  snack bar cafetería (f)
snow nieve (f)
soap jabón (m)
socks calcetines (m)
soft (bed) blando/a
  (texture) suave
sole (shoe) suela (f)
  (fish) lenguado (m)
some unos/as
  someone alguien
  something algo
  sometimes a veces
son hijo (m)
soon pronto
sore doloroso/a
  sore throat dolor de garganta (m)
sorry! ¡perdón!/¡lo siento!
soup sopa (f)

south sur (m)
South Africa Sudáfrica
South African sudafricano
South America Sudamérica
South American sudamericano/a
souvenirs regalos (m pl)
spade pala (f)
Spain España
Spanish español/a
spanner llave inglesa (f)
spare part recambio (m)
spare tyre rueda de repuesto (f)
spark-plug bujía (f)
to speak hablar
special especial
speciality especialidad (f)
speed velocidad (f)
  speed limit velocidad máxima (f)
to spell escribir/deletrear
to spend gastar
spicy picante
spinach espinaca (f)
spine espina dorsal (f)
splinter astilla (f)
sponge esponja (f)
  (cake) bizcocho (m)
spoon cuchara (f)
sport deporte (m)
spot (medical) grano (m)
  (place) sitio (m)
to sprain torcer
spring primavera (f)
square (shape) cuadrado/a
  (in a town) plaza (f)
stadium estadio (m)
staff personal (m)
stain mancha (f)
  stain remover quitamanchas (m)
stairs escaleras (f pl)
stall (market) puesto (m)
  (theatre) butaca (f)
stamp sello (m)
to start empezar
  (car) arrancar
starter motor de arranque (m)

station estación (f)
stationer's papelería (f)
to stay quedarse/alojarse
steak bistec (m)
to steal robar
steering-wheel volante (m)
sterling libra esterlina (f)
sticking plaster
   esparadrapo (m)
stiff neck tortícolis (f)
sting picadura (f)
stocking media (f)
stomach estómago (m)
stop (bus) parada (f)
to stop parar
store (small) tienda (f)
   (large) almacenes
   (mpl)
straight recto/a
   straight ahead todo recto
   straight away en seguida
straw paja (f)
strawberry fresa (f)
street calle (f)
student estudiante (m/f)
suede ante (m)
sugar azúcar (m)
suit traje (m)
suitcase maleta (f)
summer verano (m)
sun sol (m)
   to sunbathe tomar el sol
   sunburn quemadura de
      sol (f)
   sunglasses gafas de sol (f
      pl)
   sunshade sombrilla (f)
   sunstroke insolación (f)
sun-tan lotion bronceador
   (m)
supermarket supermercado
   (m)
supper cena (f)
supplement suplemento (m)
suppository supositorio (m)
sure seguro/a
surgery (doctor's)
   consultorio (m)
   (operation) cirugía
   (f)
surname apellido (m)
sweater suéter (m)

sweet dulce
   (dessert) postre (m)
sweets caramelos (m pl)
sweet corn maíz (m)
sweetener edulcorante (m)
sweetshop confitería (f)
to swell hinchar
to swim nadar
swimming natación (f)
   swimming costume traje
      de baño (m)
   swimming pool piscina
      (f)
   swimming trunks
      bañador de caballero
      (m)
switch interruptor (m)
to switch on encender
to switch off apagar
swollen hinchado/a
symptom síntoma (m)
syrup (medicine) jarabe (m)
   (fruit) almíbar (m)

T
table mesa (f)
table-cloth mantel (m)
to take llevar/tomar
talc polvos de talco (m pl)
tall alto/a
tampon tampón (m)
tap grifo (m)
tape cinta (f)
tart tarta (f)
tax impuesto (m)
   tax free libre de
      impuestos
taxi taxi (m)
   taxi rank parada de taxis
      (f)
tea té (m)
   teaspoon cucharilla (f)
   tea towel trapo de cocina
      (m)
teacher profesor/a
telegram telegrama (m)
telephone teléfono (m)
   telephone box cabina
      telefónica (f)
   telephone directory guía
      telefónica (f)   157

to telex   mandar un telex
television   televisión (f)
   (set)   televisor (m)
to tell   decir
temperature   temperatura
   (f)
   (fever)   fiebre (f)
tennis   tenis (m)
   tennis court   pista de tenis
   (f)
tent   tienda de campaña (f)
terrace   terraza (f)
test   examen (m)
   (medical)   análisis (m)
thank you   gracias
that   ese (m)/esa (f)/eso (m)
theft   robo (m)
then   entonces
there   allí
thermometer   termómetro
   (m)
thick   grueso/a
thief   ladrón/a
thin   delgado/a
thing   cosa (f)
to think   pensar
   (to believe)   creer
to be thirsty   tener sed
this   este(m)/esta (f)
those   esos (m pl)/esas (f pl)
thousand   mil
thread   hilo (m)
throat   garganta (f)
through   a través
   no through road   calle sin
   salida (f)
ticket (train/bus)   billete (m)
   (cinema)   entrada (f)
   (shopping)   recibo (m)
   (parking)   multa (f)
   ticket office   taquilla (f)
tide   marea (f)
tie   corbata (f)
tights   pantis (m pl)/
   leotardos (m pl)
time (clock)   hora (f)
   (general)   tiempo (m)
timetable   horario (m)
tin (can)   lata (f)
tin-opener   abrelatas (m)
tip (money)   propina (f)
tired   cansado/a

tissue (handkerchief)
   pañuelo de papel (m)
to   a/hacia
toast   tostada (f)
tobacco   tabaco (m)
tobacconist's   estanco (m)
today   hoy
toe   dedo del pie (m)
together   juntos/as
toilet   servicio (m)
   toilet paper   papel
   higiénico (m)
toll   peaje (m)
tomato   tomate (m)
tomorrow   mañana
tonic water   tónica (f)
tonight   esta noche
tooth   diente (m)
   toothache   dolor de
   muelas (m)
   toothbrush   cepillo de
   dientes (m)
   toothpaste   pasta de
   dientes (f)
   toothpick   palillo (m)
torch   linterna (f)
total   total (m)
tour   excursión (f)
tourist office   oficina de
   turismo (f)
towel   toalla (f)
town   ciudad (f)
   (small)   pueblo (m)
   town hall   ayuntamiento
   (m)
toy   juguete (m)
tracksuit   chándal (m)
traffic   tráfico (m)
   traffic light   semáforo (m
   traffic warden   guardia d
   tráfico (m/f)
train   tren (m)
transfer (bank)
   transferencia (f)
to translate   traducir
translator   traductor/a
to transport   transportar
travel   viaje (m)
   travel agency   agencia de
   viajes (f)
traveller's cheque   cheque d
   viaje (m)

tree árbol (m)
trolley carrito (m)
trousers pantalones (m pl)
to try probar
T-shirt camiseta (f)
tuna atún (f)
Turkey Turquía
turkey pavo (m)
Turkish turco/a
turn (in road) curva (f)
to turn (a corner) doblar
twice dos veces (f pl)
type clase (f)
typewriter máquina de
    escribir (f)
typical típico/a
tyre neumático (m)/rueda
    (f)

ugly feo/a
umbrella paraguas (m)
uncomfortable incómodo/a
unconscious inconsciente
uncooked crudo/a
under debajo (de)
underdone (meat) poco
    hecho/a
underpants calzoncillos (m
    pl)
understand comprender
underwear ropa interior (f)
United States Estados
    Unidos
unleaded sin plomo
until hasta
up arriba
upset (angry) enfadado/a
upstairs arriba
urgent urgente
use usar
useful útil

vacancy habitación libre (f)
vacation vacaciones (f pl)
vaccine vacuna (f)
vacuum cleaner aspiradora
    (f)
valley valle (m)
value valor (m)

valuables objetos de valor
    (m pl)
van furgoneta (f)
veal ternera (f)
vegetable verdura (f)
vegetarian vegetariano/a
velvet terciopelo (m)
very muy
vest camiseta (f)
video machine vídeo (m)
video tape cinta de vídeo (f)
view vista (f)
villa chalet (m)
village pueblo (m)
vinegar vinagre (m)
visa visado (m)
visit visita (f)
to visit visitar
voice voz (f)
voltage voltaje (m)
to vomit vomitar

W
to wait esperar
waiter camarero (m)
waiting-room sala de espera
    (f)
waitress camarera (f)
to wake (up) despertar(se)
Wales Gales
walk paseo (m)
to walk andar
wall pared (f)
wallet cartera (f)
walnut nuez (f)
to want querer
ward (hospital) sala (f)
wardrobe armario (m)
to wash lavar
    to wash the dishes fregar
        los platos
washable lavable
wash-basin lavabo (m)
washing-up liquid
    lavavajillas (m)
washing machine lavadora
    (f)
washing powder detergente
    (m)
wasp avispa (f)
watch reloj (m)

159

watch strap ·correa de reloj (f)
water agua (f)
watermelon sandía (f)
water-skiing esquí acuatico (m)
watt vatio (m)
weak débil
weather tiempo (m)
  weather forecast boletín meteorológico (m)
wedding boda (f)
week semana (f)
weekday día laborable (m)
weekend fin de semana (m)
weight peso (m)
to weigh pesar
welcome bienvenido/a
well bien
  well done bien hecho/a
Welsh galés/esa
west oeste (m)
wet mojado/a
what que/como
where donde
which cual/que
while mientras
white blanco/a
who quien
why por qué
wide ancho/a
wife mujer (f)/esposa (f)
to win ganar
wind viento (m)
window ventana (f)
  shop window escaparate (m)
windscreen parabrisas (m)
  windscreen wiper limpiaparabrisas (m)
wine vino (m)
winter invierno (m)
with con
without sin
witness testigo (m/f)
woman mujer (f)
wood (material) madera (f)
  (forest) bosque (m)
wool lana (f)

word palabra (f)
work trabajo (m)
to work (person) trabajar
  (machine) functionar
work permit permiso de trabajo (m)
world mundo (m)
to worry preocuparse
  don't worry ¡no se preocupe!
wound herida (f)
to wrap envolver
wrapping paper papel de envolver (m)
wrist muñeca (f)
to write escribir
writing paper papel de cart (m)
wrong (mistaken) equivocado/a

X
X-ray (department) radiografía (f)
X-rays rayos X (equis) (mpl)

Y
yacht yate (m)
year año (m)
yellow amarillo/a
yes sí
yesterday ayer
yet aún
  (already) ya
yoghurt yogur (m)
you (informal) tú
  (formal) usted
young joven
youth hostel albergue juvenil (m)

Z
zebra crossing cruce de cebra (m)
zip cremallera (f)
zoo zoo (m)